D1516367

Pilcher's

MARIJUANA
MISCELLANY

Pilcher's

MARIJUANA
MISCELLANY

STORIES, TECHNIQUES, TIPS
& TRIVIA OF THE WORLD'S
BEST-LOVED HERB

BY TIM PILCHER
WITH E. M. FROST

ILEX

PILCHER'S MARIJUANA MISCELLANY

First published in the UK, US, and Canada in 2014 by
ILEX
210 High Street
Lewes
East Sussex BN7 2NS
UK
www.ilex-press.com

Publisher: Alastair Campbell
Creative Director: James Hollywell
Managing Editors: Nick Jones & Natalia Price-Cabrera
Specialist Editor: Frank Gallaugher
Assistant Editor: Rachel Silverlight
Commissioning Editor: Zara Larcombe
Art Director: Julie Weir
Designer: Lisa McCormick
Picture research: Katie Greenwood

British Library Cataloguing-in-Publication Data
A catalog record for this book is available from
the British Library.

ISBN: 978-1-78157-141-5

Printed and bound in China

Color Origination by Ivy Press Reprographics

2 4 6 8 10 9 7 5 3 1

"The motion picture you are
about to witness may startle you.

It would not have been possible,
otherwise, to sufficiently emphasize the
frightful toll of the new drug menace, which
is destroying the youth of America in
alarmingly increasing numbers.

Marihuana is that drug—a violent
narcotic—an unspeakable scourge.

The Real Public Enemy Number One!"

REEFER MADNESS, 1936

GATEWAY DRUG

CANNABIS HAS LONG BEEN cited as a "gateway drug" leading users on to other narcotics. This controversial theory has yet to be proved conclusively, as equal numbers of scientific studies have shown that the consumption of cannabis can possibly predict a significantly higher risk for the subsequent use of "harder" illicit drugs, while other studies show that it can't! Many studies looked at correlation, rather than causation, which is notoriously difficult to prove.

According to the US-based National Institute on Drug Abuse (NIDA), "People who abuse drugs are also likely to be cigarette smokers. More than two-thirds of drug abusers are regular tobacco smokers, a rate more than triple that of the rest of the population."

A 2011 US–Finnish twin study revealed those who started smoking tobacco by the age of 12 were 26 times more likely to start using cannabis or other illicit drugs by age 17, compared to those who never smoked. It appears that tobacco smoking and drinking are the most powerful predictors of later use of illicit drugs. So, the true "gateway drugs" may in fact be nicotine and alcohol.

But whichever camp you fall in, the debate looks likely to rage on for sometime to come.

MARIJUANA SLANG

CANNABIS HAS A LANGUAGE all of its own. Smokers are referred to as Tokers, Stoners, Blazers, Space Cadets, Dope Headers, Vipers, Wasteoids, Potheads, and Herbalists, who then proceed to Skin-Up, Roll, or Get One On. After Blazing Away, they tend to be Wasted, Stoned, Mashed, Baked, Caned, Toasted, Annihilated, Gone, Blasted, Blunted, Battered, or simply just Irie. Some might get The Munchies (sudden hunger, for particularly sweet and/or salty snacks), or even Cottonmouth (lack of saliva creating a dry, parched sensation in the mouth), but what no one wants is The Whiteys (nausea and a panic attack).

——— FIVE BEST GLOBAL FESTIVALS ———

THERE ARE SEVERAL EVENTS THAT celebrate marijuana, where you can partake of a whole range of weed and mingle with other marijuana fans.

THE CANNABIS CUP, AMSTERDAM, THE NETHERLANDS (NOVEMBER)
Having run for over 26 years, this is the daddy of dope daze. A mixture of samplings and a music festival, the awards are considered the most prestigious in the world.
www.cannabiscup.com

HEMPFEST, SEATTLE, WASHINGTON, USA (AUGUST) With impressive crowds sometimes reaching 310,000, this is one of the largest pro-pot events in the world, despite only launching in 1991. Speakers have included Senators, Congressmen, and actor Woody Harrelson.
www.hempfest.org

NIMBIN MARDIGRASS, NIMBIN, NEW SOUTH WALES, AUSTRALIA (MAY) Full of talks and bands, this very peaceful and polite protest event draws crowds from all over the world. Despite constant run-ins with the local police the show has been running for 21 years and places a strong emphasis on fancy dress with the Ganja Fairies—"The spirit of the MardiGrass"—parade.
www.nimbinmardigrass.com

SPANNABIS, BARCELONA, SPAIN (MARCH) Attracting over 20,000 green gardeners from around the globe, this Spanish event has its own grower's competition with awards for best nutrients, tools, and growth systems.
www.spannabis.com

US CANNABIS CUP, SEATTLE, WASHINGTON, USA (SEPTEMBER)
The first US Cup was held in Denver, Colorado, in 2012, taking advantage of the new relaxed State laws, but then moved to Seattle in 2013.
www.cannabiscup.com

> "They lie about marijuana. Tell you pot-smoking makes you unmotivated. Lie! When you're high, you can do everything you normally do, just as well. You just realize that it's not worth the fucking effort. There is a difference."
>
> BILL HICKS, *American comedian* (1961–1994)

TOP FIVE STONER FLICKS

OF COURSE, IT PROBABLY HELPS to smoke a bowl before watching any of these:

UP IN SMOKE (DIR. LOU ADLER, 1978) The legendary, original, and best stoner movie of all time sees Cheech Marin and Tommy Chong get deported to Mexico and then, unwittingly, drive a van made entirely of grass back over the border to perform at the "Battle of the Bands" in L.A. while being pursued by incompetent DEA officers. This film paved the way for the buddy stoner comedy genre.

FRIDAY (DIR. F. GARY GRAY, 1995) Smokey (Chris Tucker) and recently fired Craig (Ice Cube) are a couple of homies getting stoned on a dealer's weed and watching their neighbors' antics in South Central L.A. The pair find themselves in trouble when they have to pay the dealer the $200 for the stash they lit up.

DUDE, WHERE'S MY CAR? (DIR. DANNY LEINER, 2000) Jesse (Ashton Kutcher) and Chester (Seann William Scott) are two bumbling potheads who can't remember where they left their car after a night of hard-core partying. They embark on a quest to find out what happened the previous night. They meet their angry girlfriends, whose house they trashed, an angry street gang, a transsexual stripper, and a group of aliens in human form. This film is the template for *The Hangover* (2009), and was directed by Danny Leiner, who went on to direct *Harold and Kumar go to White Castle* (2004).

HAROLD AND KUMAR GO TO WHITE CASTLE (DIR. DANNY LEINER, 2004) The next generation of Cheech and Chong, this film launched a series of stoned misadventures for Asian-American Harold (John Cho) and Indian-American Kumar (Kal Penn). They followed this up with *Harold & Kumar Escape from Guantanamo Bay* (2008) and *A Very Harold & Kumar 3D Christmas* (2011). All are worth watching for Neil Patrick Harris' cameos alone.

PINEAPPLE EXPRESS (DIR. DAVID GORDON GREEN, 2008) This very funny action/comedy sees stoner and process server, Dale Denton (Seth Rogen), and his cannabis dealer, Saul Silver (James Franco), on the run from cops and hit men when Denton witnesses Silver's boss killed. The title refers to a particularly rare strain of weed, "It's, like, the rarest. It's almost a shame to smoke it. It's like killing a unicorn. With, like, a bomb." And there are heaps of other stoner jokes throughout.

——— ETYMOLOGY: BONG (NOUN) ———

A water pipe for smoking marijuana through. Like a Shisha or Hookah Pipe, the water cools the smoke down, making it more pleasant to inhale. The term comes from Vietnam War veterans, who returned to the US with the Thai phrase, *baung*, literally meaning "cylindrical wooden tube." Soldiers even smoked weed through the barrel of their rifles.

—— HENRY FORD'S MARIJUANA MOBILE ——

MOTORCAR ENGINEER and entrepreneur Henry Ford was constantly pushing the frontiers of technology. In 1925 he told the *New York Times* that ethyl alcohol was "the fuel of the future," believing that grain alcohol derived from crops such as soybean and hemp would resolve any energy crisis. "Why use up the forests which were centuries in the making, and the mines, which required ages to lay down," he queried, "if we can get the equivalent of forest and mineral products in the annual growth of the fields?" He also foresaw that plastics would be the building material of tomorrow.

In the December 1941 issue of *Popular Mechanics* he revealed a new type of car made from blended cellulose bioplastics, derived from flax, wheat, spruce and, yup, you guessed it, hemp. The last ingredient's fiber was also used as a strengthener. Ford's vision was to "grow automobiles from the soil." The car's bodywork was supposedly ten times stronger than steel and 30 percent lighter. Ford's vision saw the benefits of hemp, both as a construction material and as a fuel, but in the 12 years it took to develop his car, the political landscape had changed, and the plant had gone from potential savior for US agriculture to vilified "Demon Weed." His experimental car never made it to the production lines, but it was the inspiration to Cheech and Chong's van made out of marijuana in their film, *Up in Smoke*.

—— BONGS ——

FIRST BROUGHT BACK FROM the Far East by Vietnam War veterans, the bong is one of the more fun ways to communally share some smoke. These contraptions involve burning a small piece of hash or grass in a bowl that sits on a narrow stalk, which is inserted into a large chamber, from where the rising smoke is inhaled.

Today, bongs come in all shapes and sizes, and you can buy ones that look like guns, ones that have water or ice cube chambers in them for a cool smoke, and even ones shaped like an alien's head with four mouthpieces, so you can all toke together.

Creativity is a key element of "bong culture" with stoners making them out of practically anything they can get their hands on, from hollowed-out fruit, Tupperware, old Nintendos, and Christmas decorations. As actor/comedian Denis Leary joked, "Remember that friend in High School, who wanted to make bongs out of everything? Making bongs out of apples and oranges and shit. One day you find your friend going 'Hey look, man, I made a bong out of my HEAD! Put the pot in this ear and suck it out of this one, go on take a hit!'"

"STOP THIS MURDEROUS SMOKE"

ON OCTOBER 16, 1933, a 21-year-old man, Victor Licata, killed his entire family of five—including the pet dog—with an axe in Tampa, Florida. The case became a cause célèbre, with the newspapers quickly blaming Licata's pot smoking as the reason for his violent rampage, with sensational, inflammatory headlines like, "Marijuana Maniac!"

The *Tampa Morning Tribune* stated in its story that "…It may or may not be wholly true that the pernicious marijuana cigarette is responsible for the murderous mania of a Tampa young man in exterminating all the members of his family within his reach—but whether or not the poisonous mind-wrecking weed is mainly accountable for the tragedy, its sale should not be, and should never have been, permitted here or elsewhere." Even the police clearly doubted that the cannabis was the cause of Licata's horrendous actions, but nevertheless, the case was quickly picked up by well known prohibitionists like Harry J. Anslinger, the head of the newly-formed Federal Bureau of Narcotics, who cited it in order to ease the passage of the 1937 Marijuana Tax Act, which effectively outlawed weed in the USA.

In fact, Victor Licata suffered from a form of early on-set dementia ("dementia praecox with homicidal tendencies"), and marijuana was not mentioned in any psychiatric reports. He eventually hanged himself in the Florida State Hospital on December 4, 1950.

Licata's story was the inspiration behind Cornell Woolrich's (AKA William Irish) 1941 pulp novel, *Marihuana*, and it was mentioned in the 1936 propaganda film, *Tell Your Children* (AKA *Reefer Madness*): "Yes. I remember. Just a young boy…under the influence of drugs…who killed his entire family with an axe."

—"HE HID IT IN THE ONE PLACE HE KNEW— HE COULD HIDE SOMETHING: HIS ASS."

W HEN CHRISTOPHER WALKEN UTTERS this immortal line in *Pulp Fiction* (1994) he's talking about his war buddy's gold watch, but such a quote could easily refer to any seasoned—or amateur—drug smuggler today. Shoving anything up your ass for the purposes of storage and/or transport could be considered pretty near the top of the wrongness scale, but when it comes to drug smuggling, the Anal Express is just the tip of the shitberg. Here are a few of the more bizarre and sometimes ingenious ways people have tried to smuggle marijuana across country lines:

In early 2013, police in Mexicali, Mexico, confiscated a cannon made out of PVC piping that was used to volley packages of marijuana across a fence into California. Its ammunition caliber was about 13 kilograms. Catapults and T-shirt cannons have also been used to air-drop weed across surprisingly large distances.

Not sure what to do with your old, obsolete games console? Why not re-enact a 2010 attempt to smuggle marijuana into New Jersey using a hollowed-out Nintendo Wii. Try to be successful this time.

Drug smugglers clearly have no respect for the dead, as evidenced by a man in Dallas who was stopped by police for running a red light and turned out to be hiding 100 pounds of marijuana in a casket in the back of his van. Luckily there was no room left for a corpse.

In May 2013 El Paso, Texas, customs workers discovered 591 pounds of marijuana stuffed into plaster figurines imported from Mexico.

At JFK airport in 2006, authorities confiscated twelve bricks of marijuana from persons unknown. Upon further inspection, it was found that the marijuana bricks were actually being used to smuggle a smaller shipment of hashish. (Apparently this ruse is sometimes used by kingpins further up the ladder in order to trick drug smuggling organizations further down the assembly line into thinking they're moving cheaper merchandise, so they'll charge less.)

While the above point at least makes business sense, this one makes no sense at all: The Drug Enforcement Administration once apprehended a traveler attempting to smuggle three bullets into Andrade, California…inside a package of weed.

In August 2013 the US Border Patrol caught a scuba diver attempting to smuggle eight pounds of herb into the country from Canada by swimming almost a mile across the St. Clair River into Michigan. This man gets extra credit for fitness and determination, if not success.

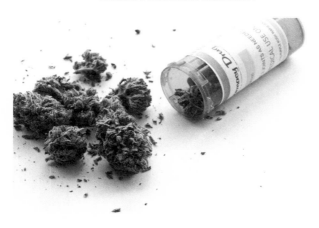

—MEDICAL MARIJUANA IN CALIFORNIA:— EASIER TO GET THAN YOU'D THINK?

MARIJUANA IS USED TO TREAT a number of medical conditions such as AIDS and cancer, as it tends to increase appetite while alleviating nausea. It's also been used with success on glaucoma patients and sufferers of Multiple Sclerosis and PTSD. Unfortunately, many of these and other possible legitimate medical uses are limited or prohibited by the criminalization of marijuana in most US states, and even accredited research scientists are finding it difficult to obtain enough weed legally to carry out properly scoped and controlled trials.

Appraised in this light, you'd be forgiven for assuming it's next to impossible to obtain a marijuana prescription in California, the first US state to legalize our herbaceous friend for medical purposes only and largely for chronic conditions. But if you're willing to bypass insurance hassles and go straight to the source (your friendly neighborhood general practitioner), local aficionados say that the cheapest and least problematic route is to claim chronic insomnia. And really, who *hasn't* had trouble sleeping at least once in their lives?

> "Is marijuana addictive? Yes, in the sense that most of the really pleasant things in life are worth endlessly repeating."
> RICHARD NEVILLE, *Writer and Co-editor of* Oz *magazine (b. 1941)*

WHAT'S IN A NAME?

CANNABIS HAS QUITE POSSIBLY MORE monikers than any other drug. Some relate to its appearance, like "Tea", or a particular strain or the location where it's grown, like "Maui Wowie." Others refer to the way of smoking it, like "Blunt" or "Bowl" (as in a the bowl of a smoking pipe). It has also gone under all of these names at some point or other: Pot, Grass, Weed, Smoke, Reefer, Mezz, Herb, Bush, Green, Mary Jane, MJ, Chronic, Spliff, Joint, Ganja, Sensei, Sinsemilla, Bud, Hemp, Dope, Draw, Kush, Hydro, Skunk, Thai Stick, Charas, Charge, Black, Hash, Hashish, Kif, Purple Haze, White Widow, Roach, Soap Bar, Bongo, Cheeba, Dagga, Diesel, Shit, Hemp, Muggles, Solid, Wacky Baccy, Gage, Stash, Sweet Leaf, and many, many more!

MULTI-CHOC-CHIP KOMA KOOKIES

BROWNIES AND COOKIES ARE THE mainstay of cannabis cooking. However, these are the best—light, soft, chewy and chocolaty, and very moorish. This recipe makes 12 large cookies.

1 cup/250g cannabutter (see page 73)	1/2 tsp baking soda
2/3 cup/125g white sugar	1/2 tsp salt
2/3 cup/125g brown granulated sugar	1 small milk chocolate bar or chips
1 large egg	1 small dark chocolate bar or chips
1 tsp vanilla extract	1 small white chocolate bar or chips
2 cups/280g plain flour	

INSTRUCTIONS:

1 Blend the cannabutter and sugars together in a bowl.

2 Beat the egg in and add the vanilla.

3 Sift the flour, baking soda, and salt in and fold into the mixture.

4 Break up the chocolate bars and sprinkle and mix them in.

5 Spread the cookie dough on a greased baking sheet and bake for around 8–10 minutes at 375F/190C.

6 Cut the baked dough into required sizes. Best served slightly warm.

———— THE HORROR OF WEED ————

A SPATE OF HORROR FILMS in the late seventies and eighties equated drug use—particularly marijuana as the teenage drug of choice—and general immorality with certain and horrible death. Horror filmmakers from the late nineties and early twenty-first century then took up that mantle and continued the cannabis carnage. Here are some of the movies that you're most likely to get murdered in if you're a stoner, or at the very least be forced to watch all your friends die:

HALLOWEEN (1978)

MOST OF THE FRIDAY THE 13TH FRANCHISE (1980–2003)

FRIDAY THE 13TH (2009 REBOOT)

POLTERGEIST (1982)

SHROOMS (2007)

SLEEPAWAY CAMP (1983)

SLEEPAWAY CAMP II: UNHAPPY CAMPERS (1988)

THE THING (1982)

THE DEVIL'S REJECTS (2005)

ZOMBIELAND (2009)

CABIN FEVER (2002)

IDLE HANDS (1999)

LAST HOUSE ON THE LEFT (1972 AND THE 2009 REMAKE)

FREDDY'S DEAD: THE FINAL NIGHTMARE (1991)

FINAL DESTINATION 2 (2003)

THE CABIN IN THE WOODS (2012)

———— HOT KNIFING ————

A LSO KNOWN AS "SPOTS" OR "BLADES," this method of smoking hash is a tad unusual. While diminishing in popularity in New Zealand and the UK—and virtually unknown in the USA—it involves heating up two large flat knives, squashing a lump of hash between them, and inhaling the rising smoke. To help funnel the smoke a bottomless glass or plastic bottle (known as a "Spottle" or "Hooter") is used. Often this is frozen to provide a cooler smoke. In 2008, six New Zealand soldiers stationed in Afghanistan were sent home in disgrace after "Spotting" hash, using a soldering iron! The fiddly nature and increased health risks (compared to using a vaporizer) mean that just 1.3 percent of regular UK tokers use this method now.

HEROES OF HEMP:
BOB DYLAN & THE BEATLES

B OB DYLAN WAS ALWAYS A STONER and was high when he recorded the 1966 track *Rainy Day Women #12 & 35* on his *Blonde on Blonde* album. The song was banned from many radio stations because of its pro-pot chorus, "But I would not feel so all alone, Everybody must get stoned."

Dylan was also responsible for switching The Beatles on to weed on August 28, 1964 at New York's Delmonico Hotel. Although George Harrison recalled The Beatles' initial encounter with cannabis, in 1960, wasn't so great: "We first got marijuana from an older drummer with another group in Liverpool. We didn't actually try it until after we'd been to Hamburg…Everybody was saying, 'This stuff isn't doing anything.'"

But Dylan's shit was on the level and The Beatles' manager, Brian Epstein, kept saying, "I'm so high I'm on the ceiling. I'm up on the ceiling." "That, for me, was the first time I smoked marijuana. And I laughed, and I laughed, and I laughed," Ringo Starr recalled.

John Lennon said, "I don't remember much what we talked about. We were smoking dope, drinking wine, and generally being rock 'n' rollers and having a laugh, you know, and surrealism. It was party time." Paul McCartney admitted that day had a profound effect on The Beatles' music, to the point that by 1969 they were singing, "Smoke pot, smoke pot, everybody smoke pot" at the end of *I Am the Walrus*.

SINSEMILLA LADY

THIS DELICIOUS AND REFRESH-ING green cocktail is sure to get the party started. First you need to make a tincture using tequila (see page 51).

15ml (1/2fl oz.) of tequila/cannabis tincture
30ml (1fl oz.) of melon liqueur
90ml (3fl oz.) of grapefruit juice
slice of melon
slice of lime
2 cherries
crushed ice

Put all of the key ingredients—the melon liqueur, tincture, grapefruit juice, and ice—into a shaker and shake vigorously. Pour the concoction into a highball glass of your choice and garnish with the melon, lime, and cherries.

INDIAN BHANG

INDIA HAS A LONG TRADITION involving cannabis. It's said that Buddha himself survived for six years by living solely on hemp seeds. Many Hindu sadhus (holy men) use cannabis, known as bhang, as a sacrament, like Rastafarians, on religious days such as the Holi festival, and to induce transcendental states.

While sadhus do smoke grass in clay pipe "chillums" many Indians and Nepalese prefer to consume cannabis by imbibing it in a drink called Bhang Ki Thandai or Sardai. This is a bit like a weed-infused lassi made with almonds, spices, milk, and sugar. The female plant and other ingredients are ground down into a paste and then boiled with milk to extract the active THC element, which is then sieved and

drunk cold. Cannabis is legal to grow and sell in India, with a permit, and is often preferred on the sub-continent to alcohol.

SMOKING ETIQUETTE

NO ONE WANTS TO BE A DRAG when sharing a joint, so here's some polite rules on how not to be rude. Generally, the person rolling blazes up first. Don't take forever skinning up, people get impatient. If you get into difficulty ask for help. Take two tokes and pass to the left, is generally the polite way to smoke in a group. Whatever you do, don't Bogart that joint! That is, don't hang onto it for ages before passing it on—take your tokes and share the wealth. Don't drool on the end of the joint, no one likes a soggy roach!

> "When I was promoting *Green Hornet*, Sony asked me to not tell too many weed stories. And I said, 'I don't think I'm capable of doing that.' It's kind of the only thing I can talk about."
>
> SETH ROGEN, *Actor and Writer (b. 1982)*

FIVE OF THE BEST AMSTERDAM COFFEE SHOPS

AMSTERDAM IS NOTORIOUS FOR ITS "Coffee shops" where you can order some supreme green to go with your latte. Either pre-rolled or DIY, different cafes stock different strains of grass and hash. Here are some of the most famous cafes, but there are plenty more off the beaten track that have fewer tokin' tourists.

DAMPKRING Made famous by a guest appearance in *Ocean's Twelve* (2004), this is one of the more traditional smoking dens with psychedelic art on the walls and a friendly atmosphere.

THE BULLDOG Admittedly the most touristy of all the cafes, but still has a good atmosphere. Originally starting in a small basement, there are now five branches across the city. Also has a five-star hostel to crash in when it all gets too much.

THE GRASSHOPPER Four floors of flaming fun, this venue not only has the essential coffee shop, but also pubs and restaurants, meaning you need never leave. All lit-up in green at night it was name-checked in The Streets' song about getting wasted in Amsterdam, *Too Much Brandy.*

BARNEY'S Recently renovated, this 23-year-old institution is now a hi-tech cafe with each table sporting a digital menu and vaporizer. It's also the home to incredible milkshakes and seven Cannabis Cup Winners, so you know the quality is good! Up by the Centraal Station, it opens at 7am. How much weed can you smoke in 18 hours before it closes again?

ROKERIJ This popular chain has cafes across the city. With their cave-like interiors, Moroccan cushions, and trance music, they're a cosy place to lose a few hours.

PERSONAL ANECDOTE:

——— NOT THE ESCAPE YOU NEED, ———
BUT THE ONE YOU DESERVE

It's hard to pin down the appeal, really. I first smoked the nasty, rubbery, sticky brown stuff called 'Soap Bar', and I daresay the nicotine in the tobacco did more for me than the dust-like motes of bastardized hashish; I started smoking cigarettes as a result of starting to smoke other things, rather than the other way around. Gear, weed, skunk, hash, whatever you've got, it helps close the door on worries, on long-term thinking, on fear of the future. For a long-term depressive, it works surprisingly well, up to a point—the point being when it becomes the focus of your life, rather than a little help to get through it. But then the same is true of every other drug.

——— HIGH TIMES ———

FOUNDED IN 1974 by activist and pioneering underground journalist Thomas King Forcade, *High Times* is a US counterculture magazine that celebrated all manner of illicit highs. Forcade was an underground journalist, activist, and drug smuggler, and this latter role provided the title's financial backing. The erratic Forcade often pitted staff against each other and even fired the entire team, rehiring them all the next day. The magazine hit a zeitgeist and in just four years had reached a circulation of 420,000 (rivalling *Rolling Stone* and *National Lampoon*) when Forcade committed suicide in 1978. His lawyer friend Michael Kennedy picked up the reigns and shifted the magazine's focus away from LSD, mushrooms, and cocaine, and on to marijuana.

It soon became synonymous with sinsemilla, starting the infamous Cannabis Cup in Amsterdam, which was established by Steve Hager in 1987, who was then made Editor-in-Chief of the publication the following year. Since then the magazine has branched out into a number of other awards, as well as festivals, filmmaking, book publishing and even a compilation album of Herbal Hip-Hop songs (*High Times Presents THC Vol. 1*). 2007 even saw a controversial reality TV series, *High Times Office.*

The magazine itself has featured a roster of impressive contributors including authors Charles Bukowski, Truman Capote, Samuel R. Delany, and Hunter S. Thompson, cannabis activist Ed Rosenthal, and reggae star Peter Tosh.

SHE TRADED HER BODY FOR DRUGS— AND KICKS!

Marijuana Girl

N. R. DeMexico

B328
35¢
K

NEVER WAS THERE SO OUTSPOKEN A NOVEL AS THIS... TELLING THE PLAIN, UNCENSORED TRUTH ABOUT TEEN-AGE ADDICTS — AND THEIR DESPERATE SEARCH FOR THRILLS!

PERSONAL ANECDOTE:

KNOW YOUR LIMITS

AT THE RIPE AGE OF 28 or so, I found that I was still capable of proving myself to be a buffoon. This lesson, like many others throughout my life, came at the expense of both my health and my pride—and I blame weed. Mostly.

I was invited to a close friend's tropical-themed summer barbecue party and when we arrived in his sister's huge, landscaped garden, we were met by women in bikinis with cold beers. Being hungry, my friend and I both grabbed a handful of brownies as soon as we sat down and washed them down with beer. As the surrounding friends and family giggled, we were informed that they had been "magic" brownies.

That was no concern to hearty men such as us! Still hungry, and the with the barbecue food taking far too long, I grabbed another handful of brownies. I had enough experience of smoking and ingesting weed between festivals, college, and a trip to Amsterdam to know my limits. Yet after about 30 minutes it was clear that something was wrong.

When I got double-vision, I decided to go splash my face with cold water. This should have been easy enough, but the trip to the bathroom was somewhat more difficult than normal since I could no longer feel my legs. I found the stairs and gripped the banister for dear life. Halfway to the summit, I was sweating profusely. I could feel all the blood draining from my cranium down to my ineffectual, heavy legs. Reaching the top, I staggered to the bathroom, closed the door behind me, and half-turned, half-fell on to the bathroom sink. I swallowed all the water I could and then sat down on the floor.

A chunk of time escapes me, but I drifted between being asleep and being lucid. Finally, I dragged myself up and out of the bathroom. Moving was now much easier, although oddly I could now not feel any part of my body, just a warm glow. I felt like an angel as I floated into the kitchen where my friend's sister was. Taking me by the hand, she led me to a sofa bed, lay me down, and covered me with a blanket. She began to unlace my sneakers. "No!" I squealed in a falsetto far removed from my normal voice, "No! Not my feet! Don't take my feet! I *need* them!"

I awoke the next day with what can only be described as the worst headache ever crapped out of Satan's butt and into a human's head. Dehydrated, frail, and aching, I finally spoke to other guests and discovered that most of the brownies were indeed weed brownies, but some had been *amphetamine* brownies.

THE TIMES, THEY ARE A CHANGIN'

WE'VE COME A LONG WAY in the 77 years since marijuana was first made illegal in the USA with the 1937 Marihuana Tax Act. November and December 2012 saw two States take a vote on whether to legalize cannabis. Both Colorado and Washington State voted 55 percent in favor of marijuana reform, making it legal to grow, possess, and sell grass, under license. It remains illegal for anyone under 21, and to grow without a license. These landmark events have since spurred on other states to reconsider their marijuana laws; however, Oregon voted against it. Former US president Jimmy Carter was a long-standing advocate for decriminalization and legalization, and was delighted to "let the American people see" how well it works. Consultants estimate that annual marijuana sales could top $495 million in over 300 licensed stores across Washington alone.

ETYMOLOGY: MARIJUANA (NOUN)

The actual etymological origins of the word marijuana stem from the Mexican Spanish *marihuana*, but before that the trail goes cold. Some have postulated that it comes from the Spanish proper name *Maria Juana* or "Mary Jane," but the truth is, no one really knows for sure.

——— HERO OF HEMP: SETH ROGEN ———

PROBABLY ONE OF THE MOST SUCCESSFUL stoners that Hollywood has ever known (or at least, that we know of), actor/writer/producer/director/comedian Seth Rogen is a household name—and his name is indelibly linked to weed.

As a filmmaker, Rogen has made stoner movies not only acceptable, but massive money-making enterprises: witness *Pineapple Express* (2008), *This Is the End* (2013), *50/50* (2011), *Superbad* (2007), and *Knocked Up* (2007). As an actor, he most often plays the loveable stoner, and he does it extremely well—most likely a result of the massive amounts of research he's been doing for the role his whole life. Instead of shying away from pot's place in his creative process, he's always been very honest about using the drug as a creative tool: "I smoke a lot of weed when I write, generally speaking," said Seth Rogen to HighRoulette.com in 2013. "I don't know if it helps me write. It makes me not mind that I'm writing. And I don't know if it makes me work better, but it makes me not care that I'm working. Who wants to work? But if you're stoned, it doesn't seem like work."

Apart from Rogen's personal use, his films have made smoking a mainstream endeavor, taking the once fringe-genre "stoner movie" and turning it into a Hollywood cash cow. Money being the catalyst it is, that alone has probably done more for public acceptance than any amount of political lobbying.

> "There was no time to weigh chances. There was no such thing as chances anyway, in the distorted perspective of the weed fumes."
>
> CORNELL WOOLRICH, *Marihuana (1941)*

— DOES THE PUNISHMENT FIT THE CRIME? —

SPURRED BY THE BLANKETING WAR ON DRUGS, marijuana has been lumped in with other far more dangerous drugs in the USA, morally and legally. Despite the recent rash of states legalizing marijuana possession for personal use, it is still a federal crime, and often the jail sentences doled out for possessing small amounts of marijuana are completely disproportionate to the offense.

In the United States, marijuana is classified as a Schedule I drug, along with heroin and other opiates, and is grouped with hallucinogenics such as LSD, mescaline, and PCP. (For comparison purposes, the "less harmful" Schedule II is comprised of Methamphetamines and cocaine.) As such, simple possession and low-level dealing can carry some of the heftiest jail terms available, and according to the FBI, almost 50 percent of all drug arrests in the US are for marijuana. In 2010, Oklahoma mother-of-four Patricia Spottedcrow was sentenced to 12 years behind bars for selling $31 worth of pot, her first criminal offense. A year later, Patrick Carney of Covington, Louisiana, received a 30-year sentence for selling $25 worth of marijuana, after previous convictions for cocaine possession and second-degree battery all resulted in probation. Some US states have decriminalized or legalized marijuana possession, but many still prescribe jail terms and high fines for possessing even small amounts:

IDAHO demands up to a one-year jail sentence and $1,000 fine for personal use possession of three ounces or less (more than three ounces and you're looking at a felony charge with up to five years in jail and a $10,000 fine).

In OKLAHOMA, a first-offense of possession in any amount carries a one-year jail term; a second offense in any amount carries two-to-ten years.

GEORGIA considers any amount over one ounce a felony, punishable with up to ten years in jail.

For possession of less than 20 grams, FLORIDA charges as a misdemeanor with one year of jail time and a $1,000 fine. Over 20 grams and it's a felony carrying five years imprisonment or a $5,000 fine.

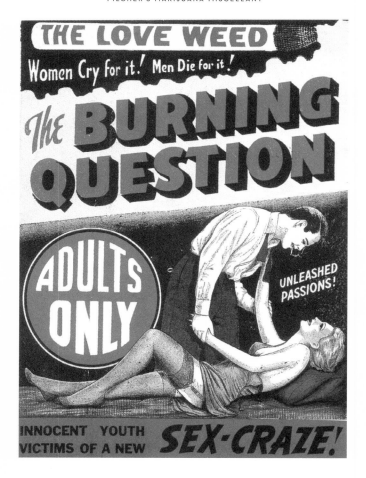

------- ETYMOLOGY: DAGGA (NOUN) -------

South African term for Cannabis Indicia and Sativa. Derived from
Afrikaans and the Hottentot word, *dachab,* circa 1670–1675.

PERSONAL ANECDOTE:

FIRST-TIMER'S FOLLY

THE FIRST TIME I TRIED POT, it had been home-grown on a rooftop in New York's Lower East Side by a family of urban hippies, and every stereotype you've ever heard of came true. First, the munchies. I was at a house party brimming with chips and dips, so I took myself over to the snack table and literally started stuffing Doritos into my mouth as fast as I could. Honestly, I'm not even sure I was hungry—I just needed food to be in my face right away. Then came the absolute certainty that everyone was staring at me. I wasn't paranoid enough to stop eating, but when I wasn't guiding my hand to the bowl I was darting glances around the room trying to catch the eye of anyone who might be looking in my general direction. The hunger and the paranoia probably only lasted about 15 minutes, followed closely by the bliss. Worth it.

"Weed's not as bad as everything else, cause weed is a background substance. You know what I mean, you can smoke some herb and still function. You ain't crisp…but you'll function."

DAVE CHAPPELLE, *Comedian (b. 1973)*

POISON!

MARIJUANA HAS HAD A LONG and troubled history with respect to the law, most often because it's been automatically equated with far more addictive and destructive drugs such as opium, cocaine, and meth, as well as it being habitually mislabeled as a narcotic.

In the early 1920s, Egypt was experiencing a significant hashish problem among its population, and prevailed upon the League of Nations to criminalize the drug and help slow international traffic. The Egyptian delegate at the 1925 Geneva Opium Convention called hashish "a dangerous narcotic" and "more harmful than opium," and asserted that most lunatics in Egyptian asylums were hashish abusers. He asked for global controls prohibiting the import/export of cannabis, or Indian Hemp, and cannabis was duly sanctioned alongside opium and opium derivatives, except for medical and scientific purposes. As a result, Britain rescheduled cannabis as a poison effective from April 1925. Thankfully it didn't last.

——— HEROES OF HEMP: WILLIE NELSON ———

COUNTRY AND WESTERN singer, Willie Nelson is the co-chair of the National Organization for the Reform of Marijuana Laws (NORML) and has sat on its advisory board for over a decade, fighting for marijuana legalization. In 2005 he hosted the first annual Willie Nelson & NORML Benefit Golf Tournament, which led to an appearance on the cover of the January 2008 issue of *High Times* magazine.

When Nelson's lung collapsed while swimming in 1981, and after suffering several bouts of pneumonia, he decided to quit either marijuana or tobacco—he chose the latter. In 2008 he started using a vaporizer to ease the strain on his lungs.

He has been arrested several times for possession of marijuana. The first was in 1974 in Dallas, Texas, then 20 years later in 1994, he was busted for a single marijuana cigarette in his car near Waco, Texas. On his way to a funeral in 2006, Nelson was busted yet again—this time in Louisiana—and charged with possession of marijuana and hallucinogenic mushrooms. He received six months probation. On November 26, 2010, Nelson was arrested in Sierra Blanca, Texas, for possession of six ounces of marijuana found in his tour bus. He was released on a $2,500 bail. After this last arrest he set up the TeaPot party.

In his 2012 autobiographical musings, *Roll Me Up and Smoke Me*

When I Die, the 80-year-old Nelson explained, "I thought, 'Hey there's a Tea Party, so why not a TeaPot Party?' There are now TeaPot Party representatives in every state of the union, and even in several foreign countries. On a few occasions, the TeaPot Party has backed a few politicians who believe, as we do, that marijuana should be legalized, taxed and regulated."

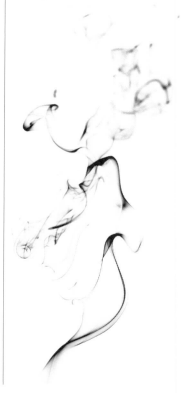

—— THE EMPEROR WEARS NO CLOTHES ——

POSSIBLY THE MOST IMPORTANT BOOK to be written about cannabis in the 20th century is Jack Herer's *The Emperor Wears No Clothes*. Published in 1985, it was the first book to investigate the real reasons why such a profitable and prodigious crop such as hemp was outlawed around the world. Herer was a late convert to cannabis, but became an ardent campaigner for its legalization, establishing Help End Marijuana Prohibition (HEMP). The book explores how hemp has been systematically erased from the collective consciousness as an indispensable, cheap, and plentiful tool for making paper, rope, clothes, cattle feed, and even plastics.

While the late Herer is seen as a bit of a hero in the cannabis counterculture (there's an award-winning strain of weed named after him), there are some European crop experts, like Dr. Hayo M. G. van der Werf, who think some of his claims about hemp as a panacea for the world's problems were grossly exaggerated. Ironically, *The Emperor Wears No Clothes* may be just that. However, there is still an unclaimed $100,000 reward for anyone who can disprove his research.

—— CANNABIS CONSUMPTION ——

DESPITE BEING EFFECTIVELY illegal in nearly every country in the world, cannabis nevertheless remains the third most popular drug, after tobacco and alcohol. The 2012 *UN Drug Report* estimated that 180.6 million people enjoyed cannabis that year, that's 3.9 percent of the world's population aged 15–64. And it's on the increase.

In America it's estimated that over 70 million people have tried it, and one in 12 adults and teenagers smoke it at least once a year. The USA has also seen the amount of outdoor cultivated plants that have been destroyed by authorities rise from 213,000 in 2002, to 462,000 in 2010—more than double! And like the UK, more is being homegrown than imported. However, production of hashish in Morocco and Afghanistan has dropped slightly in recent years. Despite that, the French Ministry of the Interior estimates that 80% of the resin consumed in Europe comes from the Rif region in Morocco.

> "It really puzzles me to see marijuana connected with narcotics, dope, and all that crap…it's a thousand times better than whiskey. It's an assistant—a friend."
>
> LOUIS ARMSTRONG, *Musician (1901–1971)*

GEORGE AND CHARLOTTE GO TO WHITE CASTLE

L OVE IT OR LOATHE IT, it's standard scientific procedure to test new (and old) drugs on animals before progressing to human trials. The average citizen is far more enlightened about the unethical exploitation of animals now more than ever before—if only because of the plethora of real-time information we find ourselves bombarded with on a daily basis—so there are certain methods of research that we just won't countenance from the scientific community anymore. Despite this, scientists are still getting up to some strange shenanigans; here are a couple that involve marijuana, and not necessarily for the betterment of humankind:

In 1995, NASA thought it'd be a great idea to get spiders high on a variety of drugs and then see what kind of webs they wove. It *was* a great idea, and predictably the pothead spider gave up weaving his web about halfway through to wander off in search of Pringles. (Conversely, the LSD webs showed remarkable precision and intricacy.)

In 1974, the Heath/Tulane study set out to prove the adage that marijuana use kills brain cells. The study indicated that its test subjects, rhesus monkeys, were forced to inhale the equivalent of 30 joints a day; after 90 days they died and were found to have severe and permanent brain damage. It wasn't revealed until much later that the monkeys were actually administered daily doses of the equivalent of 63 joints through gas masks *in five minutes*. This means that every day the monkeys were deprived of oxygen for a full five minutes and the brain damage they suffered was due to suffocation, not marijuana. To this day there is no evidence that weed causes brain damage, permanent or otherwise.

HEROES OF HEMP: SOMA

THIS DREADLOCKED US-born herbal horticulturist started growing marijuana back in 1971. In 1996 he moved to Amsterdam where he set up his renowned Soma Seeds company, offering his award-winning seeds in the post to aspiring growers. He specializes in growing organic grass and medical marijuana, particularly after having open-heart surgery in 2005, and self-medicates with his own crops, prescribing 10–15 grams a day. He has won both the Cannabis Cup and the IC Growers cup three times, and 2007's Spannabis Champions Cup, and lectures as a "Ganja Guru" while regularly contributing to many magazines.

TOP TEN POT FICTION

MARIHUANA BY WILLIAM IRISH
(Dell, 1941)

REEFER BOY BY HAL ELLSON
(Pedigree, 1957)

THE MARIJUANA MOB BY JAMES
HADLEY CHASE *(Eton, 1952)*

MARIJUANA GIRL BY N. R.
DEMEXICO *(Beacon, 1960)*

REEFER GIRL BY JANE MANNING
(Cameo, 1953)

MARIJUANA MURDER BY
ANONYMOUS *(Superior, 1946)*

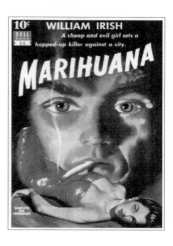

IT AIN'T HAY BY DAVID DODGE
(Dell, 1946)

SEX, POT AND ACID BY GEORGE
BAILEY *(Viceroy, 1968)*

REEFER CLUB BY LUKE ROBERTS
(Stallion, 1953)

DOPE, INC. BY JOACHIM JOESTEN
(Avon, 1953)

VENDING MACHINES

WE'RE AWARE THAT JUST THE concept of vending machines that dispense marijuana sounds like something only possible in a fantasyland where rainbows only have endings and unicorns roam freely across fields growing Twizzlers instead of grass, but this is serious. They exist.

With these vending machines already in use in medical dispensaries in the US, courtesy of California-based company Medbox Inc., other businesses are hoping to get in on the game and capitalize on weed's legality in Colorado and Washington. This probably doesn't mean we'll be seeing weed machines in every mall in America anytime soon, but it's very possible that a few years down the line, weed stores where the drug is legal will offer the automated option alongside the personal sales touch, and customers can choose according to their preference (and just for future reference, vending machines have already been designed to sell edible pot treats as well as pure bud).

COMEDY CANNABIS SONGS

BY THE GIGGLES IT INDUCES, it's no wonder there are plenty of funny marijuana tracks. Here's three of the best:

SOAP BAR BY GOLDIE LOOKIN' CHAIN *(Straight Outta Newport, 2004)*
The Welsh rappers spat lyrics extolling the joys of smoking cheap-ass hashish with this number: "Soap Bar's cheap, and so's my clothes, They've got to be cause of all the fucking holes, It tastes like shit and it makes you cough, And it's the fucking rubber in it that gets you off."

THE REEFER SONG BY MINDLESS DRUG HOOVER *(Top Banana, 1997)*
This bizarre folky acoustic little ditty tells the tale of a cyclist who gets arrested and then proceeds to get the entire police station wasted: "Well I sold them two ounces and one 16th, and they rolled the biggest joint the world had ever seen…" Terribly remixed by The Orb.

BECAUSE I GOT HIGH BY AFROMAN *(Because I Got High, 2000)*
Despite being a humorous track about a man whose entire life is destroyed by smoking dope, this song became a huge hit, reaching No. 1 in nine countries. It was the theme tune for Kevin Smith's film *Jay & Silent Bob Strike Back* (2001), and he went on to direct the music video.

WEST SIDE WEED

THE 1957 SONG *Gee, Officer Krupke*, from one of the best-loved musicals, *West Side Story*, had some very controversial cannabis-related lyrics by Stephen Sondheim:

Dear kindly Judge, your Honor,
My parents treat me rough.
With all their marijuana,
They won't give me a puff.

My father is a bastard,
My ma's an S.O.B.
My grandpa's always plastered,
My grandma pushes tea.

These original stage lyrics were changed slightly for the film version, but nevertheless kept the subtle nods to marijuana and "tea," which then later caused it to be banned by the BBC in 1962 because of the scandalous drug references. Years later, Sondheim stated he originally wanted it to be the first Broadway show to use the words "fuck" and "shit" in its song lyrics, with the end of the song being "Gee, Officer Krupke, Fuck you!" but in the end, the producers succeeded in softening it to "Krup you!"

HEROES OF HEMP: MR. NICE

HOWARD MARKS AKA "Mr. Nice," is the world's most notorious ex-cannabis smuggler. At his height he was smuggling 30 tons of weed into the USA hidden inside a fictional rock band's speakers.

After making various connections in the early seventies, the Oxford graduate was soon smuggling hashish from Afghanistan, Lebanon, and Pakistan into Germany, Ireland, and the UK. By 1972 he was making £50,000 on each shipment. Regarding his smuggling as a service he deliberately avoided hard drugs recalling, "A dealer is really just someone who buys more dope than he can smoke. And I have to say, I'm ashamed, I tried to smoke it all. There was just too fuckin' much of it."

As Marks recalled in his autobiography, *Mr. Nice*, "Between 1975 and 1978, 24 loads totaling 55,000 pounds of marijuana and hashish had been successfully imported through John F. Kennedy Airport, New York. They had involved the Mafia, the Yakuza, the Brotherhood of Eternal Love, the Thai army, the Palestine Liberation Organization, the Pakistani Armed Forces, Nepalese monks, and other individuals from all walks of life. The total profit made by all concerned was $48,000,000. They'd had a good run."

Incredibly, the Welshman made contacts with the IRA, MI6, and the CIA, with the latter even setting up a $300,000 cannabis deal with Marks. Unfortunately, it all went wrong when the contact died and US Customs seized the haul.

In 1988 he was eventually caught by the US Drug Enforcement Agency, extradited from Spain to the States, and was sentenced to 25 years in a maximum security prison, but released after seven in 1995.

Now a writer, public speaker, activist, and occasional DJ, Marks (who lives up to his moniker) is a leading voice in the demand for the legalization of grass in the UK, and even stood for Parliament in the 1997 UK elections. His book was adapted into a 2010 film, also called *Mr. Nice*, and he was played by fellow Welshman, Rhys Ifans.

MAKING HASH

TAKING THE STICKY CANNABIS resin formed by the trichomes (glands) of the female plant, hashish can be made in one of three ways. Firstly, dried buds are sieved—either mechanically or by hand—through gauze and the residue powder is heat compressed into blocks. The second method involves filtering the buds with iced water. This allows the precious trichomes (which contain the active THC) to sink to the bottom while the leaves and stalks float. The residue is then filtered to purify it further, and is known as "bubble-hash." This is because you can test the purity of the hash by adding heat to it. The more it bubbles, the better the quality. The final method is to chemically extract the resin using solvents like ethanol, which is then evaporated, and forms a "honey oil" or "hash oil," but purists tend to avoid this method as the process breaks down the trichomes. The trouble with hash is that many unscrupulous dealers cut it with various adherents to stretch the product further. Notorious "Soap Bar" has been known to contain everything from plastics to engine oil, and even faeces. So just make sure your shit is good shit and not shit shit.

> "The illegality of cannabis is outrageous, an impediment to full utilization of a drug which helps produce the serenity and insight, sensitivity and fellowship so desperately needed in this increasingly mad and dangerous world."
>
> CARL SAGAN, *Astrophysicist (1934–1996)*

4:20

ALSO WRITTEN AS 420, this mysterious number has long been a secret code for tokers. Many theories have developed about its origins, from being the number of various legal acts and bills, or amount of active chemicals in cannabis, to even the date of Bob Marley's death (actually May llth, 1981), but none of these are true. The real origin of these curious digits way goes back to the early seventies in San Rafael, California when a bunch of stoner students, known as "the Waldos," needed a code for arranging a smoking session. The number referred to the time, 4:20pm, so fellow stoners could pass in the corridors saying "420, [insert location]?" without fear of being busted. The phrase spread virally until in became common parlance, a decade later, for asking if someone had weed or to simply identify a fellow smoker. Nowadays it's associated with April 20th as an unofficial date to celebrate weed.

PICK YOUR HIGH

Although cannabis grows in three main strains—sativa, indica, and ruderalis—herbal horticulturists have spent decades constantly mixing and matching genetic strains, looking for the perfect high, tailored to smokers' requirements. For example, Strawberry Cough has a fruity flavor to it, while Purple Kush produces a heavy and mellow high. These are seeded from either sativa, indica, or a blend of the two.

Breeding requires pollinating a female plant with male pollen. The males —identified by their ball-like stamen—are separated from female plants to prevent accidental fertilization and to allow more control over which male is used. The selected male pollen is then sprinkled on the female flowers. The resultant seeds have the characteristics of both plants. It's a tricky business as the seeds can often be infertile. If this is the case then crossbreeding needs to be stabilized by "cubing." This process involves finding specific traits in the new hybrid plant (such as increased resin production) that match traits in a stable parent plant and then breeding the two. This process sometimes needs to be repeated two or three times (hence the term cubing) before the strain is stable enough to breed by itself.

Today there are hundreds of strains to pick from, including Super Silver Haze, Northern Lights, Kryptonite, Champagne, Shiskaberry, Big Bud, White Widow, Western Winds, Kali Mist, G13, and endless Skunk varieties. The list continues to expand as farmers seek new ways to get people stoned.

HEROES OF HEMP: ROB VAN DAM

American professional wrestler Rob Van Dam has been a vocal proponent of the use and legalization of weed for the entirety of his 20-plus-year career. Even an arrest for 18 grams of marijuana in 2006 has not deterred him; if anything, it's made him more determined to fight for pot's cause.

In addition to occasionally contributing opinion pieces to *Cannabis Culture* magazine, he's incorporated the 4:20 aesthetic into his merchandize and was featured in *High Times* magazine in 1999.

When most high-profile wrestlers were hiding their habits in shame, afraid of the drug-using athlete stigma, Van Dam spoke out about the medicinal benefits, physical and mental, of cannabis, and even claimed that marijuana makes him a better athlete. In 2009 he spoke at the NORML National Conference, and he continues to advocate smoking in the media at every opportunity. For his tireless campaigning on behalf of this medicinal of herbs, Rob Van Dam takes his well-earned place among the exalted Heroes of Hemp.

—————— ACRONYM: CDB ——————

The second most active cannabinoid in marijuana, cannabidiol (CDB) is thought to act as a counterbalance to its more psychoactive cousin, THC. Its sedative effect means that potential medical uses include easing epilepsy, spasms, anxiety disorders, bipolar disorder, and schizophrenia. Research has even shown that it helps halt the growth of cancer cells.

US STATES WHERE CANNABIS HAS BEEN DECRIMINALIZED

21 STATES HAVE NOW MADE medical marijuana legal, and the following states have decriminalized the plant, which isn't the same as legalizing it, although two states have: Colorado and Washington.

1 COLORADO *(legal)*

2 CONNECTICUT

3 MAINE

4 MASSACHUSETTS

5 MINNESOTA

6 MISSISSIPPI

7 NEVADA

8 NEW YORK

9 NORTH CAROLINA

10 OHIO

11 OREGON

12 RHODE ISLAND

13 VERMONT

14 WASHINGTON *(legal)*

DAMNED IF YOU DO, DAMNED IF YOU DON'T

ON THE RECREATIONAL DRUG scale of harm, marijuana is perceived to be at the lowest end, causing the fewest negative side effects while having a high positive value to the user. The drug's ability to calm is probably the most cited reason for use, so it's no surprise that many people with anything from daily stress to diagnosed anxiety disorders choose to self-medicate with weed. But for all its soporific qualities, marijuana can also cause anxiety and, in particular, panic attacks. In fact, anywhere from 20 to 30 percent of smokers report having panic attacks after smoking. The mechanics of weed's ability to cause anxiety isn't yet understood—it could be genetic or it could be that many smokers have anxiety problems to begin with—but it seems that first-timers are the most susceptible. Novices take note: always use the buddy system. Safety first.

> "Some people are just better high."
> JUSTIN TIMBERLAKE, *Musician (b. 1981)*

MARIJUANA AS A (POTENTIAL) CHEMICAL WEAPON

IN THE 1960S, US ARMY Colonel Dr. James Ketchum conducted experiments involving marijuana and mind control at the Edgewood Arsenal in Maryland. Edgewood was the headquarters of the US Army Chemical Corps, and Chief of Clinical Research Ketchum intended to build a new kind of chemical weapon, one that would incapacitate the enemy without immediate damage or long-term harm—most likely by sending them to sleep for an extended period or inducing almost paralyzing attacks of the giggles. Ketchum dreamed of a "war without death," and used a highly potent, synthetic form of marijuana to try to achieve it.

The subjects of the Army experiments were soldiers who volunteered, and the trials were conducted under rigorously controlled scientific conditions. One potent THC compound and one stereoisomer produced satisfying effects: the compound caused a volunteer to find everything funny and have trouble raising his arms, and the stereoisomer effected a significant drop in blood pressure, causing the subjects to faint and have trouble moving. Unfortunately, in Ketchum's opinion, the Army decided a sudden drop in blood pressure could be dangerous and suspended trials, thereby eliminating the possibility of a non-lethal, marijuana-based chemical weapon.

'CAUSE I GOTTA HAVE DOPE

GEORGE MICHAEL, CANNABIS, AND CARS have never been a good combination.

One of the biggest pop stars of the past 30 years, Michael has unfortunately been in the press on numerous occasions for combining two pastimes that really don't mix; smoking marijuana and driving. On February 26, 2006, he was found slumped at the wheel in Cricklewood, North-West London, after motorists reported a car obstructing the road at traffic lights. He was arrested for possession of Class C drugs, calling the incident "my own stupid fault, as usual." He pleaded guilty on May 8, 2007 to driving while unfit through drugs. He was banned from driving for two years and sentenced to community service.

During the radio show *Desert Island Discs* in September 2007, he admitted that his cannabis smoking was a problem and he was trying to cut down. But he added he didn't think it was "getting in the way of my life in any way... I'm a happy man and I can afford my marijuana so that's not a problem." By December 2009 he told *The Guardian* newspaper that he had reduced his intake from 25 joints a day to a mere "seven or eight" spliffs per day. Still impressive by anyone's standards and he even described himself as "the poster boy for cannabis."

The Careless Smoker was then arrested in September 2008 for possession of Class A and C drugs in a Hampstead Heath public toilet, but was let off with a caution.

Unfortunately, he was busted again, in the early hours of Sunday July 4, 2010, when he drove into a storefront in Hampstead, North London and was promptly nicked for being unfit to drive. He was "charged with possession of cannabis and with driving while unfit through drink or drugs." He pleaded guilty and was given a £1,250 ($2,000) fine, a five-year ban from driving, and sentenced to eight weeks in prison (serving four). "This was a hugely shameful thing to have done repeatedly," he recalled, "So, karmically I felt like I had a bill to pay. I went to prison, I paid my bill."

After suffering from a three-week coma induced by pneumonia in 2012, Michael finally foreswore the wacky baccy. Unfortunately, that wasn't the end of the stoned singer's car-related calamities, as in May 2013 he fell out of a friend's moving Land Rover on the M1, sustaining head injuries, but recovered. Here's hoping his marijuana motorway mishaps are now behind him.

> "I believe in individual rights. I mean, I would like
> to see everybody be able to smoke pot."
>
> SUSAN SARANDON, *Actress and Activist (b. 1946)*

—————— HOLY COW HOT CHOCOLATE ——————

THIS IS SIMPLY DELICIOUS, even without the holy herb added.

1 cup/250ml milk
5 tbsp granulated sugar
1 cup/250ml single cream
pinch of ground cinnamon
½ tsp vanilla extract

⅛oz/4g cannabis finely ground
5oz/150g plain chocolate
1 small chocolate bar,
whipped cream and/or baby
marshmallows to decorate

INSTRUCTIONS:

1 Gently heat the milk and sugar in a pan until the sugar dissolves. Then add all the other ingredients, apart from the chocolate and other toppings.

---

2 Bring to the boil, then simmer for abut one hour. Then pour the resulting "cannamilk" through a coffee filter.

---

3 Put the cannamilk back in the pan, break up the chocolate, drop it in, and gently heat until melted, stirring all the time.

---

4 Pour into a mug and decorate with whipped cream, marshmallows and grated chocolate. Yum!

Personal Anecdote:

— ADVENTURES IN WEEDLAND —

MY FIRST EXPERIENCE OF MARY JANE—solid, not the really good stuff, that came later—was at a house party thrown by one of my new high school friends. I'd only been in the area for about three months, and at the high school for two. It was a Friday night, and one of my first social engagements since moving to north London. It was a typical north London, mid-nineties party full of overly emotional teenage girls and ridiculously aloof not-quite-men. Mostly those in attendance were from my school—there were a few random girls and some ultra-crusties from the local boys' school there as well, which was not a turn of events that went down particularly well with the aloof not-quite-men, leading to laughable pubescent posturing on both sides. Incidentally, that night was also the first time my new school friends discovered that I really don't take kindly to emotional teenage girls insulting people and emptying bottles of what I fervently hoped was water over anyone unlucky enough to be within striking distance. Not long after catching and explaining to one of those girls why that is simply not acceptable behavior, one of the random girls broke out the solid and a fancy little rolling machine. "Darling," she said, while she very slowly and deliberately laid the ingredients onto the machine and cranked the handle, "Fuck the spoiled little bitches. Have some of this." And with that one sentence, she changed my life.

I should point out that while this might sound like it took just a matter of seconds, anyone that's ever smoked single skins from a rolling machine and then shared that single skin with several other people will know that it actually took upward of 20 minutes. So myself and three or four other girls basically held our own incredibly slow, mini-smoking party. We were suitably impressed with the little roller, and at one point, someone actually compared the joint appearing fully formed to having a baby. Eventually, the machine birthed enough tiny joints for us all to be quite wrecked and then we were all sent off with a tiny joint of our own.

I retired to the lounge and the group already settled there weren't too happy—mostly they objected to my smoking a joint. Not from a legal standpoint weirdly, but from a health one. Two of the ordinarily much cooler boys from my year spent several minutes attempting, unsuccessfully, to talk me out of it. Not long after that, the non-smokers dispersed and left the stoners to a far more pleasant party, thus setting up a pattern that would continue for many, many happy years.

RELIGION

DESPITE PREDOMINANTLY being associated with Rastafarianism and Coptics, many religions have used marijuana in rituals. Japanese Shintoism celebrates hemp as a symbol of purity, with offerings of the plant (along with rice and salt) made to the divine Kami. Shinto priests wave a gohei wand made of hemp fibers over worshippers dressed in hemp paper robes in an act of cleansing. Small government-sanctioned plantations also exist where the hemp is grown to supply temples with sacred rope and other materials for these rituals. The Middle Eastern Sufis also regard cannabis, or kaif, as sacred and use it in a similar way as Rastafarians—as a means of communicating or getting closer to Allah. Other religions connected to the use of marijuana include Tantric Buddhism, Hinduism, and ancient Pagan rituals.

SKUNK

THE MOST NOTORIOUS STRAIN of weed, Skunk has a strong, heady aroma, hence the name. Mostly grown hydroponically, the Sativa-dominant weed has a much higher THC level (10–15 percent) than other strains and very little CBD. This is great for getting that instant head rush and a very strong high, but the lack of the CBD has caused some concerns for heavy smokers. Some scientists believe that ingesting high levels of THC encourages schizophrenia and other mental disorders. There are at least 11 different sub-strains of Skunk, including Cheese, Amnesia, and the slightly ominous-sounding Deathskünk.

COMPLETE LIST OF CANNABIS CUP WINNERS

1988—SKUNK #1
by Cultivator's Choice

1989—EARLY PEARL/SKUNK #1
X NORTHERN LIGHTS #5/HAZE
*by the Seed Bank, Snocap by David
Swenson*

1990—NORTHERN LIGHTS #5
by the Seed Bank

1991—SKUNK BALLS
by Free City

1992—HAZE X SKUNK #1
by Homegrown Fantasy

1993—HAZE X NORTHERN
LIGHTS #5
by Sensi Seed Bank

1994—JACK HERER
by Sensi Seed Bank

1995—WHITE WIDOW
by Green House

1996—WHITE RUSSIAN
by De Dampkring

1997—PEACE MAKER
by De Dampkring

1998—SUPER SILVER HAZE
by Green House

1999—SUPER SILVER HAZE
by Green House

2000—BLUEBERRY
by the Noon

2001—SWEET TOOTH
by Barney's

2002—MORNING GLORY
by Barney's

2003—HAWAIIAN SNOW
by Green House

2004—AMNESIA HAZE
by Barney's

2005—WILLIE NELSON
by Barney's

2006—ARJAN'S ULTRA HAZE #1
by Green House

2007—G-13 HAZE
by Barney's

2008—SUPER LEMON HAZE
by Green House

2009—SUPER LEMON HAZE
by Green House

2010—TANGERINE DREAM
by Barney's

2011—LIBERTY HAZE
by Barney's

2012—FLOWER BOMB KUSH
by Green House

HEROES OF HEMP: KEVIN SMITH

KEVIN SMITH HAS NEVER SHIED away from speaking about his special relationship with marijuana. He claims he didn't become a "hard-core stoner" until after *Zack and Miri Make a Porno* bombed at the box office (2008)—apparently he was introduced to pot in a serious way by Seth Rogen—and some critics mark that moment as the beginning of the end of his filmmaking career. However, Jay and Silent Bob were dealers in *Clerks* (1994), Smith's fictional comic-book characters Bluntman and Chronic appeared in *Chasing Amy* back in 1997 and became an actual comic book written by Smith in 2001, and his comic store in New Jersey is called Jay and Silent Bob's Secret Stash, which could be a euphemism for…something. Whatever his actual history with the drug, Smith has stated publicly that heavy smoking has focused his work ethic and actually increased his creative output, which goes some way to dispelling the slacker myth. Maybe.

TEN CLASSIC GRASS STRAINS

(By strength)

1 JACK HERER *****

2 SAGE****

3 WHITE WIDOW****

4 YUMBOLDT****

5 WARLOCK HAZE****

6 SILVER HAZE****

7 WHITE RUSSIAN***

8 AK-47***

9 BUBBLEGUM***

10 K2**

PAPERS

THE MOST POPULAR way of smoking marijuana is by rolling a joint, for which you need good rolling papers, or skins. In the bad old days this would involve gluing together small papers (78mm long) to make a doobie worth smoking, but eventually manufacturers caught on and started making king-size versions, around 100mm long, which made skinning up that much easier. These days there's an endless variety to choose from, including flavored (liquorice, grape, and banana), rolls (such as Rips) that allow enormous joints to be created, pre-rolled cones that you just fill with gear, and even honey-dipped tobacco leaves for rolling blunts. Of course, aficionados use only hemp paper to roll their own.

HARRY J. ANSLINGER

IF THE STORY OF MARIJUANA has a single villain it's Harry J. Anslinger. An ardent anti-drug campaigner ever since he heard the screams of a morphine addict at the age of 12, Anslinger was made Assistant Prohibition Commissioner in the Bureau of Prohibition. Promoted to Commissioner of the Federal Bureau of Narcotics in 1930, he was alarmed by the growing use of cannabis as a possible replacement for opiate abuse, and made it his mission to make marijuana illegal. It was already restricted in several states, but Anslinger set about with a zeal to have it banned on a Federal level.

He teamed up with William Randolph Hearst's newspapers, creating a scare campaign, using cases like Victor Licata, who axed his family to death—supposedly under the influence of marijuana. He warned, "Marihuana is a shortcut to the insane asylum. Smoke marihuana cigarettes for a month and what was once your brain will be nothing but a storehouse of horrid specters. Hasheesh makes a murderer who kills for the love of killing out of the mildest mannered man who ever laughed at the idea that any habit could ever get him…" He ran radio campaigns and even supported the making of Dwain Esper's sensational 1935 cannabis exposé, *Assassin of Youth*.

He was also a blatant racist, using his discrimination as a reason for pot prohibition, "Colored students at the Univ. of Minn. partying with (white) female students, smoking [marijuana] and getting their sympathy with stories of racial persecution. Result: pregnancy…" He actively targeted jazz musicians in his campaign, seeing several arrested for possession, including Gene Krupa and Louis Armstrong.

Eventually, in 1937, Anslinger's hate campaign against hemp succeeded with the passing of the Marijuana Tax Act, which effectively outlawed cannabis in America. Not resting on his laurels, he also managed to convince other countries to join the ongoing prohibition. Having spent 32 years railing against weed, he finally retired in 1962 and passed on to the Great Bureau in the Sky on November, 14, 1975. His vilifying policies did more harm to the harmless stoner than any other politician or government body before or since.

"I went to Vietnam, and I was there for a long time…
[Using marijuana] made the difference between staying human or,
as Michael Douglas said, becoming a beast. I'm telling you, it's rough
and a lot of people in that platoon used it, not on the front line
but in the back, to stay in touch with themselves."

OLIVER STONE, *Director (b. 1946)*

THE FABULOUS FURRY FREAK BROTHERS

THE PERENNIAL STONER TRIO of Phineas, Freewheelin' Franklin, and Fat Freddy (and not forgetting the latter's cat), first appeared in 1968 when creator Gilbert Shelton drew them for the Texan underground paper, *The Rag*. Inspired by the Marx Brothers and the Three Stooges, Shelton printed 3,000 copies of the first comic and sold a few hundred in Austin before heading to San Francisco, the then home of underground comix, to sell the rest and set up Rip Off Press publishing company.

Initially, the strips were just about everyday pothead concerns, like getting high, getting laid, claiming welfare, and trying to avoid being arrested by narks (narcotics officers). But Shelton, assisted by Paul Mavrides and Dave Sheridan, started more ambitious storylines creating multi-part, globe-spanning epics like *Grass Roots*, where the boys find a "year's supply" of cocaine and move to the country with the proceeds, and *The Idiots Abroad*.

There have been numerous attempts at transferring the tokin' triad to the big screen, either as live action or, most recently in 2008, as claymation. But as yet none has been successful. Knockabout, The Freak Bros.' UK publisher since the late seventies, released an Omnibus in 2008 that collected every single trippy strip to date, even the rare color one that appeared in *Playboy*.

The 14 comics have remained almost continuously in print for over 40 years, with the three unrelated "brothers" still entertaining thousands of stoners with every new generation that discover them. There is an unfinished Freak Brothers story set on a houseboat in Amsterdam with the aged trio, and Shelton has said, "…Perhaps one of these days we'll get back on that project, especially if we can find a way to hire a couple of dozen more artists." But with it being over 100 pages, and Shelton's increasing age, it's looking unlikely.

10 CLASSIC HASHISH TYPES

(By strength)

1 NEPALESE TEMPLE BALLS*****

2 MELANA CREAM*****

3 ROYAL NEPALESE*****

4 JELLYHASH*****

5 NORTHERN LIGHTS****

6 WHITE WIDOW****

7 SUPER KETMA****

8 AFGHANI BLACK****

9 GOLD LEBANESE***

10 SHEEBA***

A MYSTERY EVEN MYSTERY, INC. COULDN'T SOLVE

TECHNICALLY, THEY'RE THE ONLY ONES who *could* solve it, but they're not talking. Children's TV of the 70s and 80s ran the gambit from subversive to outright trippy, but the most overt alleged allusion to marijuana use has to be Norville Rogers—better known as "Shaggy"—from the cartoon *Scooby Doo*. He, along with his constant companion Scooby, just had that vibe of the habitual smoker about him. But those involved with the show—including radio legend Casey Kasem, who voiced Shaggy for twenty-five years—maintained he was just a goofy product of the times. Fans have always wondered, though, especially after they grew up and were able to make more informed connections. On the one hand, Shaggy's portrayed as your garden-variety hippie slacker—long haired, shabbily dressed (bell bottoms!), and a bit slow on the uptake. On the other hand . . . well, let's look at the evidence, shall we?

EXHIBIT A: Shaggy is from a town called Coolsville. Literally, that is actually the town he's from. This may or may not have anything to do with him being an alleged smoker, but it needs to be said. *Coolsville.*

EXHIBIT B: "A bit slow on the uptake" could equate to a bit stoned. Shaggy often seems to have no idea where he was or how he got there, a little surprised about what was going on but on the whole okay with it. In other words, he's high.

EXHIBIT C: Shaggy and Scooby clearly live in the back of a van. A Mystery Machine, no less. It's like a magic carpet ride but smoother and a little low-rent.

EXHIBIT D: Shaggy and Scooby constantly have the munchies. They are shoving food in their faces 24/7 like Doritos are going out of style. What's that about weed increasing appetite?

EXHIBIT E: Shaggy says "like," like, all the time. Because that's what happens, like, when people's brains are moving at, like, one-fifth of their normal, like, speed and they need to punctuate the, like, silence to make it sound like they're still, like, paying attention.

EXHIBIT F: Um . . . what were we talking about?

There will probably never be a clear answer to whether Shaggy was a stoner, because he was and is, after all, the star of a children's show. But to be honest, we'd all be a bit disappointed if any of the creators came out and said he was, because it's much for fun to have our own mystery to solve. And we would solve it, too, if it weren't for those meddling kids!

ALL THAT JAZZ

L ONG BEFORE REGGAE AND RAPPERS became associated musical champions of wacky baccy there was another group of performers who were inspired by the marijuana muse: jazz musicians. Known as "tea" in the twenties, thirties, and forties, grass was inspiring Cab Calloway to sing about "that funny reefer man" in 1932. Another jazz term for a stoner or grass was a viper, and in 1938 Sidney Bechet & Noble Sissles Swinster's sang "I'm viper mad."

Between 1943–1950 The Narcotics Bureau attacked the jazz scene and lots of musicians were arrested in the crackdown, including drummer Gene Kruper—who received a three-month jail sentence for just two joints—and Louis Armstrong, who was lucky enough to get off with a suspended sentence. Armstrong was a vocal proponent of the herb even recording his 1928 paean to it, *Muggles* (slang for marijuana) and he wrote in his memoirs, "It really puzzles me to see marijuana connected with narcotics…dope and all that crap. It's a thousand times better than whiskey—it's an assistant—a friend."

But the king of them all was Milton "Mezz" Mezzrow. The clarinetist/saxo-phonist was arrested in 1940 for possession of 60 joints entering a jazz club, with intent to supply. He became such a renowned dealer to fellow musicians that his name became synonymous with marijuana, and he was immortalized in Stuff Smith and the Onyx Boys' classic, *You'se a Viper*: "Dreamed about a reefer, Five foot long, The mighty Mezz, but not too strong, You'll be high, but for long, Cuz you'se a viper…"

MARIJUANA TINCTURE

WHILE THE THC IN MARIJUANA can be broken down in fats and oils, it can also be extracted in alcohol, and consequently powerful cocktails await those who are prepared to put the effort into making a tincture. Here's how.

YOU'LL NEED:

3/4oz/22g Marijuana leaves and/or buds

3floz/90ml of 40–70% proof alcohol

Something sweet, like a peach schnapps or a brandy, is better than vodka, to hide the bitterness

Muslin or a coffee filter

Funnel

Dark green, blue or brown glass bottle with an airtight screw lid

INSTRUCTIONS:

1 Grind up the marijuana into a fine powder and soak overnight in warm water. This removes any water-soluble impurities while leaving in the THC.

2 The following morning, drain off the water using the muslin/coffee filter and scoop the damp powder into the glass bottle and pour the alcohol on top.

3 Give it a good shake and store the bottle in a cool, dark place for ten days, and shake daily. After ten days it's ready to use, but the longer you leave it, the stronger it gets.

4 Then filter the grass out with the muslin/coffee filter, keeping the liquid and discarding the now inert grass. You can repeat steps 1–3 again with fresh cannabis to increase the potency, but I wouldn't!

5 You can drink the tincture straight or add it to a cocktail, or use in cooking.

MAHJOUN

IN THE 11TH CENTURY, Middle Eastern Arabs were prevented by Islam from drinking alcohol. However, they were allowed to consume cannabis, so they took lumps of hashish, dried fruit, nuts, and honey, and pulverized it into a sweet sticky treat known as mahjoun. The recipe spread all over the Arabic world, including Morocco, where it was sometimes made with alternative ingredients of small doses of the narcotic plants datura and belladonna, and butter and gum Arabic.

THE MUNCHIES: SCIENCE OR PSYCHOLOGY?

THERE IS AN OVERWHELMING AMOUNT of anecdotal evidence suggesting that marijuana use increases appetite, so much so that the phenomenon has been given a name all of its own: "the munchies." While it's been theorized that the munchies is a psychological side-effect of smoking—the drug lowers inhibitions and gluttony is often at the top of the vice list—there is in fact a physiological basis for the marriage of marijuana and Taco Bell.

It was previously believed that marijuana, like all drugs, acted primarily on the brain and so if the munchies were in fact a physical response to smoking, it would be because it changed the perception of how food tastes by bonding to the appropriate brain receptors. But a recent study by the Monell Chemical Senses Center in Philadelphia, Pennsylvania, and Kyushu University in Japan has found that the cannabinoids in weed—which ape the naturally occurring, appetite-inducing endocannabinoids in the body—directly affect the taste buds, making foods seem sweeter to the smoker.

The Monell Center believes that this breakthrough in roach research could pave the way to new methods of treating obesity, diabetes, and lost appetite as a result of other diseases. If you needed yet another argument for the legalization of medical marijuana, you're welcome. Pay it forward by writing to your local government representative or moving to California.

THE CANNABIS CUP

GROWING WEED is its own reward, but for the truly serious herbal horticulturists there's only one event that really counts, The Cannabis Cup in Amsterdam. The music and marijuana festival is held in November every year and hundreds of growers from all over the world gather and bring their strains of weed that they've been nurturing to be judged in what is the stoner equivalent of The Chelsea Flower Show. Launched in 1987 by activist and *High Times* editor, Steve Hager the show allows anyone to pay to become a judge, with the highest number reaching 2,300 in 2008. Having run for over a quarter of a century, 2012's winner was Flower Bomb Kush, an incredibly fast-growing strain that flowers in five-and-a-half weeks instead of the average eight, and was described by one of the judges as "strong Kush taste similar to Purple Kush and nice couch lock high…that shit was booooom!" April 2013 saw the first US iteration of The Cannabis Cup take place in Denver, Colorado, with 15,000 people turning up, revealing how lax the American law has recently become on all things marijuana.

HOW TO ROLL A JOINT

THERE'S A MILLION DIFFERENT WAYS to skin-up and as always creativity rules. For the novice you'll need some cigarettes, a lighter, some king-size rolling papers, some thin cardboard and, of course, some hash or grass!

1 If mixing with tobacco (advisable for newbies) run a flame down a cigarette to dry the tobacco out. Then lick your finger and run it down the length of the cigarette and tear the moist strip off allowing the contents to drop onto the king-size paper. Alternatively, simply hold the cigarette upside down and gently roll it between your fingers and let the tobacco sprinkle out over the paper.

2 Tear off a thin strip of cardboard and roll it up tightly and place at one end of the paper. This is the "roach." You can buy pads of ready-to-roll roach paper, or the more health conscious may want to use a filter instead.

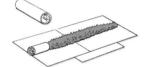

3 Grind up your grass as small as possible so that it burns evenly, or heat the hash with a lighter so that it crumbles easily, and then sprinkle along the length of the joint.

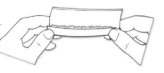

4 Gently pick up the paper and roll it between your forefingers and thumb, taking care not to drop the contents on the floor.

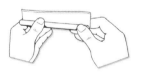

5 Carefully lick the gummed strip of the paper—make sure it's not too wet (no one likes a soggy joint and it won't light)—and roll over and seal it. Don't pack it too tight, as air needs to flow through.

6 Twist the end, light, and enjoy!

Note: *This can take years of practice to get it just right!*

RASTAFARIANISM

THE "SACRED 'ERB" or ganja, is a central tenant of the Rastafarian religion, and Rastafarians believe that smoking weed purifies the body and mind, bringing them closer to Jah (God). Using the Bible as the justification for toking, they quote many passages including: *Genesis 1:29* "And God said, Behold, I have given you every herb-bearing seed, which is upon the face of all the earth, and every tree, is the fruit of a tree yielding seed; to you it shall be for meat;" *Genesis 3:18* "…thou shalt eat the herb of the field;" and *Psalms 104:14* "He causeth the grass to grow for the cattle, and herb for the service of man," among others. As they point out, weed is a gift from God.

Rastas use ganja (from the Sanskrit, *ganjika*) in two main ways. Reasoning involves one honored member lighting up and passing the sacrament round while matters of Jah are discussed. The joint, or chalice, is passed clockwise, except in times of war when it's passed in the opposite direction. The other time grass is taken is on holy days known as Groundation or Binghi, such as July, 23—their spiritual leader, Haile Selassie's birthday. These are marked by days of singing, feasting, dancing, and smoking.

The use of marijuana has caused much conflict for Rastas over the years, seeing them persecuted across the globe. In 1998 Janet Reno, the US Attorney General, said that Rastafarians did not have the religious right to smoke grass, and in the UK this ban apparently does not contravene the European Convention on Human Rights. However, the more progressive Italian Supreme Court changed their laws in 2008, allowing Rastafarians larger possessions of ganja for sacrament.

"I've been smoking weed for forty-four years, five nights a week… I'm the poster boy to prove it doesn't do you much harm."
LEE CHILD, *Writer (b. 1954)*

—AFTER-SCHOOL SPECIAL: JUST SAY NO!—

ALMOST EVERY AMERICAN WHO WAS a tween or teen between the early seventies and late nineties will be well-versed in the After School Special oeuvre, but here's a little run-down to get the younger—or older—kids up to date. Over 25 years, ABC produced a series of melodramatic made-for-TV movies aimed at educating the youth about the dangers of being young. Topics given the teen treatment included divorce, death, illiteracy, peer pressure, and, of course, drugs.

Stoned, broadcast in 1980 and starring heartthrob-to-be Scott Baio, starts off as a primer in how to smoke, with good-boy Baio choking on some joint smoke and then graduating quickly to a bong (mostly unlit). He quickly gains friends, confidence, giggles, and game, but loses interest in school. He's warned that "marywana" causes chromosome damage, birth defects, and sterility (according to a "government survey"), but Baio just doesn't take the hype seriously, and continues on his path of self-destruction. After he almost kills his brother in a rowboat accident due to grass-induced negligence (but ends up only destroying his hopes and dreams instead), Baio sees the error of his ways and sets the bong aside.

Stoned takes a different tack than the usual gateway drug malarkey fed to children of a certain era, in that it focuses on the dangers of using drugs to escape adolescent problems. But the real moral here is clear: friends don't let friends row stoned.

—————SMUGGLING'S A NO-NO—————

EVER THOUGHT ABOUT "DOING A HOWARD MARKS" and smuggling harmless weed around the world? Here's a list of countries you should *definitely avoid* trafficking in, as they all carry the death penalty. Some countries like China and Thailand are avid executioners, whereas others, like the Philippines, repealed the death sentence in 2006.

Saudi Arabia	China
Malaysia	United Arab Emirates
Indonesia	Thailand
Singapore	Egypt

Technically, the USA reserves the right to execute anyone trafficking over 60,000 kilos, or 60,000 plants, but thankfully this law has never been enforced. In June 2013, British pensioner, Charles Ferndale, was sentenced to be hanged for smuggling in three tons of cannabis (worth $4.6/£2.9 million) into Egypt from Pakistan, along with four others. You have been warned!

SOUTH AFRICA

I N SOUTH AFRICA CANNABIS is known as "Dagga," and it grows from the border of Mozambique, in the North, all the way down the Eastern Cape to Port Elizabeth. South Africa preempted America's prohibition of grass by banning it in 1928, but regardless, this "Green Gold" is the main source of income for thousands of people. Today, Dagga is sold in various ways from wraps, called "fingers," bags known as "bankies," in matchboxes, and tied up in "Malawi cobs" (similar to Thai sticks), and it's incredibly cheap by US standards. A whole kilo can cost as little as 90 rand (£6 or US$10).

Local strains like the legendary Durban Poison (with its uplifting cerebral high), Malawi Gold, and Swazi Red are held in high regard by connoisseurs. But it's important not to get Dagga confused with Wild Dagga, a completely different plant, *Leonotis leonurus*, or Lion's Tail. Funnily enough this other Dagga is part of the mint family, but can also be used like cannabis, but has a weaker high, and is occasionally used as a substitute. While technically legal in the US, the smoke is supposedly unpleasant and rough, so many use the dried leaves in a minty tea. The main psychoactive component of *Leonotis leonurus* is leonurine, which acts in a similar way to THC in marijuana.

THE REAL COSTS OF AMERICA'S "WAR ON DRUGS"

I N 2010 over 656,000 Americans were arrested on marijuana charges, and on average, an American is arrested for violating cannabis laws every 30 seconds. More money is spent on law enforcement than on prevention and treatment combined. And fighting the war on drugs isn't cheap either. It costs the state of Florida $1.9 billion a year to prosecute offenders and a staggering $3 billion in New York. In 2013 the Cato Institute estimated that the US Government could save $13.7 billion a year if marijuana wasn't prohibited.

ETYMOLOGY: SINSEMILLA (NOUN)

Circa 1975, from the Mexican Spanish, *sin semilla*, literally meaning "without seed." The technique of growing cannabis where only the unpollinated female plant is allowed to blossom, without seeds being formed, thus giving large panicled flowers ("buds") that have a high content of cannabinoids.

THE SLACKER MYTH

FOR YEARS POT SMOKING has been stigmatized by "the slacker myth"—apart from all the cancers, infertility, and brain damage we've been warned about, it's been said that pot also makes you stupid, forgetful, and lazy. Stoner representation in movies has been squarely set in the "loser" camp for decades, even in films that aren't necessarily anti-marijuana. Think Jeff Spicoli in *Fast Times at Ridgemont High* (1982), Travis in *Clueless* (1995), The Dude in *The Big Lebowski* (1998), Brian in *Half Baked* (1998), and Cheech & Chong among many, many others. We're not saying they're not heroes in their own right, but these characters are usually jobless, feckless, and muddling through life limited by a cocoon of smoke.

Outside of fiction, however, some of our most productive young people are crediting marijuana for their success, at least in part. Seth Rogen smokes while he writes, and his output has been vast and of quality; pro-wrestler Rob Van Dam has won 21 championships, mostly while high; author Alexandre Dumas loved his hash; Bob Marley did all right for himself; Sir Richard Branson, he of the vast business empire, is a fan; travel guru Rick Steves is a member of the National Organization for the Reform of Marijuana Laws and credits pot with making him a better travel writer…The list of successful potheads is just too long to enumerate here.

Times are changing and with a younger generation of successful professionals speaking out about their productive relationships with cannabis, the slacker stereotype is sure to crumble. Eventually.

WEIGHTS AND MEASURES

IN THE UK MARIJUANA OFTEN GOES by the name of the amount bought. So if you were having a quiet night in you might get a sixteenth (¹⁄₁₆oz). If a few friends were popping in it's time for an eighth (⅛oz). Anything between a quarter (¼oz), a half (½oz), or an ounce is guaranteed to be more fun, but if you were having a seriously hardcore party it's time for a key (1 kilo)!

In the USA, there's different terminology. A nickel bag actually costs around $5 and a dime bag, double that. A "dub" will set you back $20, and a "30 sack," is unsurprisingly $30. A "50 piece" (AKA "an eighth") gets you three "dubs" for $50, saving ten bucks, whereas a "25," or "quarter," is $100's worth. A lid is roughly worth $200, and is often the largest amount a dealer will sell at a time. The term describes the earlier practice of estimating the measurement by simply filling up a tobacco tin all the way to the top (or, to the lid). As in "let's go score a lid."

Note, these don't tell you the actual amounts of grass you get, and that can vary based on the quality of the bud. So a dime bag of low-grade "Schwag" might mean you get 2–3 grams, whereas some hi-grade green may only be one gram.

Even if they have no dope, dealers are easily spotted by the possession of lots of ziplock bags, a small set of scales, and an inordinate amount of cash on them!

> "When you smoke the herb, it reveals you to yourself."
> BOB MARLEY, *Musician (1945–1981)*

HEROES OF HEMP: CYPRESS HILL

EVERYONE KNOWS RAPPERS love a nice toke, but the members of Cypress Hill took their love of green to new highs. With classic songs like *Hits from the Bong, Insane in the Brain, I Wanna Get High, K.U.S.H., Ganja Bus, Stoned is the Way of the Walk, Dr. Greenthumb*, and cover versions of *I Love You Mary Jane* and *Legalise It* all dedicated to their favorite herb, there's no doubting where the West Coast rappers stand on the marijuana debate.

The Latino rock hip-hoppers—currently consisting of DJ Mugs, B Real, Sen Dog, and Eric Bobo—became the officially recognized spokesmen for the National Organization to Reform Marijuana Laws (NORML) back in 1991. They even set up their own successful pro-cannabis Smokeout Music Festival in San Bernardino, California in 1998, which is meant to cater specifically to medical marijuana patients.

"When I was in England, I experimented with marijuana a time or two, and I didn't like it and didn't inhale and never tried it again."
BILL CLINTON, *Former US President (b. 1946)*

—————— GUERRILLA GARDENING ——————

A FRAID OF GROWING GRASS in the garage and getting grabbed by the cops? A safer alternative is guerrilla gardening! Marijuana is a strong, hardy plant that grows practically everywhere—it's not called "weed" for nothing! This makes it ideal for planting in those out-of-the-way hidden places that no one ever goes to, like deep woods or uncultivated fields in the middle of nowhere. The advantage of this is that no one can connect you with the crop unless you're caught harvesting it. The disadvantage is that any stoner can come along and steal it, or worse, the cops could confiscate it. This happened on August 24, 2013, when British police discovered 90 plants growing in the heart of the Norfolk Broads' 116-square mile National Park. However, as PC Paul Bassham pointed out, "In June last year 60 plants were found growing in an area off the River Bure close to Ranworth Broad." Once grass starts to self-seed, it's very hard to get rid of!

Some cheeky guerrilla gardeners have even gone so far as to sow the seeds of dissent in public flower beds outside police stations. If you're going to protest, say it with flowers!

"But let me get to the point, let's roll another joint."
TOM PETTY, *Musician (b. 1950)*

———— "LEGALIZE IT!"—OH, YOU HAVE ————

DESPITE GROWING ON EVERY CONTINENT on the planet (well, with the obvious exception of Antarctica) marijuana is illegal in practically every country on Earth. In fact the only country where it's completely and 100% legal to grow, smoke, and sell cannabis is, ironically, North Korea, where it's regarded as a plant, not a drug. However, you are free to smoke in the places listed below, which have either made it legal or decriminalized personal possession of small amounts. Note: decriminalization means different things in different places. Sometimes it's simply accepted public policy that police forces won't expend resources pursuing small-time possession. Other places it means a fine, but not a criminal conviction. Check with locals before toking!

ARGENTINA *(Decriminalized)*

AUSTRALIA *(Decriminalized in South Australia, Australia Capital Territory, Western Australia, and the Northern Territory only)*

BELGIUM *(Decriminalized)*

CAMBODIA *(Legally de facto)*

CANADA *(Medical marijuana with permit only)*

COLUMBIA *(Decriminalized)*

COSTA RICA *(Decriminalized)*

CROATIA *(Decriminalized)*

CZECH REPUBLIC *(Decriminalized)*

ECUADOR *(Decriminalized)*

ESTONIA *(Decriminalized)*

FRANCE *(Medical marijuana with permit only)*

INDIA *(Legally de facto in certain states only)*

MEXICO *(Decriminalized)*

NEPAL *(Legally de facto)*

NETHERLANDS *(Decriminalized)*

NORTH KOREA *(Legal)*

PAKISTAN *(Legally de facto)*

PERU *(Decriminalized)*

PORTUGAL *(Decriminalized)*

SPAIN *(Decriminalized)*

SWITZERLAND *(Decriminalized)*

URUGUAY *(Legal for personal use only)*

USA *(Legal in Washington and Colorado states only. Decriminalized in 14 other states. But watch this space! Many other states have legalization on their agenda.)*

— HASH —

THE DARK BLOCKS of what is known as hash originated in India and the Arab world as early as The Bronze Age (think 3000–1000 BC) and were used as a medicine, either eaten or smoked in a pipe. The name derives from the Arabic for grass (hashish) and is also known as Charas in the Sub-continent. Today hash often goes by the name of its origin and color, such as Lebanese Red, Afghani Black, or Moroccan Brown. The different colors depend on the types of farming, manufacture, and ways of storing it. Hash slowly loses its THC content over time, as it oxidizes, so the fresher the better!

MEDICAL MARIJUANA

THE MEDICINAL USE OF CANNABIS has been around since Ancient Egypt (as a treatment for sore eyes) and China, when Emperor Shen Nung recorded its use in 2737 BC. In India, it's thought to cure fever, dysentery, sunstroke, phlegm (it's an excellent expectorant), aid digestion, increase appetite, and even cure a lisp!

Numerous recent controlled studies have revealed that THC has mild analgesic effects and it has helped decrease tremors in a quarter of Multiple Sclerosis sufferers. There's also evidence that it helps AIDS and cancer patients by increasing appetite and decreasing nausea, and helps glaucoma patients by reducing eye pressure. In 2006, the Scripps Research Institute even discovered THC "may provide an improved therapeutic for Alzheimer's disease" and that it was "considerably more effective" than two of the leading Alzheimer's drugs on the market, donepezil and tacrine.

With new benefits being discovered all the time, it's unsurprising that the big pharmaceutical companies are now extracting THC-derivatives and putting it into pills. Yet while no one has overdosed from smoking grass, a new FDA-approved THC-laden pill, Marinol, has been linked to nasty side effects, including several deaths. Mark Kleiman, director of the Drug Policy Analysis Program at UCLA's School of Public Affairs said, "It [Marinol] wasn't any fun and made the user feel bad, so it could be approved without any fear that it would penetrate the recreational market, and then used as a club with which to beat back the advocates on the whole cannabis as a medicine." In 2005 GW Pharmaceuticals brought out a cannabinoid mouth spray called Sativex that relieves pain and spasticity in MS patients.

Another cannabinoid, cannabidiol (CBD), is thought to be the major anti-convulsant that aids MS patients, while cannabichromene (CBC) acts as an anti-inflammatory. Medical marijuana usage has been sharply on the increase in the last 20 years, and has been used to help treat everything from diabetes to Crohn's disease, and new benefits are continually being discovered. However, it still remains highly controversial with many scientists disagreeing with each other's research.

> "Penalties against possession of a drug should not be more damaging to an individual than the use of the drug itself… Nowhere is this more clear than in the laws against possession of marijuana in private for personal use."
>
> JIMMY CARTER, *Former US President (b. 1924)*

"[Marijuana] is not a drug. It's a leaf."
ARNOLD SCHWARZENEGGER, *Actor and Politician (b. 1947)*

MIDNIGHT EXPRESS

ON OCTOBER 7, 1970 an American student, Billy Hayes, was caught trying to smuggle four pounds (2kg) of hashish out of Turkey and was sentenced to four years in prison. His sentence was extended to a life sentence, and then subsequently reduced to 25 years. He eventually escaped İmralı Prison on October 2, 1975 in a rowboat and managed to get over the border to Greece. He recounted his harrowing incarceration in the book, *Midnight Express*, which was turned into a 1978 award-winning film, written by Oliver Stone and directed by Alan Parker. In the film, Hayes discusses his arrest with a shadowy American representative known as "Tex":

BILLY HAYES: I didn't have heroin. It was just a little hashish.
TEX: That doesn't matter. A drug's a drug.
BILLY HAYES: It was only two kilos.
TEX: It doesn't matter if it was two kilos or 200 kilos. The Turks love catching foreigners. They want to show the rest of the world that they're fighting the drug trade.

The film was criticized for being overly sensational, brutal, and for unfairly portraying Turkey in a particularly bad light. Hayes felt bad about this and eventually returned to the country in 2007—speaking at a conference held by the Turkish National Police—and apologized to the Turkish people.

ACRONYM: THC

Tetrahydrocannabinol is the holy grail of cannabis growing. While there are well over 60 cannabinoids naturally occurring in marijuana, each having a different effect on the human brain, THC is one of the most psychoactive, and is the one that gives stoners that buzz they're all looking for. The highest concentrations of THC are found on the trichome tips of the plant—the sticky resin that is formed. First discovered in 1964, THC causes relaxation, altered vision, hearing, and smell, and increases appetite (AKA "munchies"). But too much *may* induce paranoia and mental problems in developing brains. Interestingly, another cannabinoid, CBD, counteracts many of these problems and so it appears that weed is self-regulating. Oh and it apparently makes male mice sterile, so lay off, Mickey!

———ALICE B. TOKLAS———

Hᴵꜱᴛᴏʀʏ'ꜱ ʙᴇꜱᴛ-ᴋɴᴏᴡɴ ᴄᴀɴɴᴀʙɪꜱ ᴄᴏᴏᴋ, Alice B. Toklas, was Gertrude Stein's lover, confidante, and chef. She wrote her 1954 literary memoir, *The Alice B. Toklas Cookbook*, mixing memories with recipes, the most famous being "Haschich Fudge," a blend of fruit, nuts, spices, and cannabis. Technically, this was the North African stoner snack, mahjoun, rather than the hash brownies that she would become linked to. Ironically, Toklas didn't actually come up with the recipe herself, but was given it by her friend Brion Gysin who'd picked it up while in Morocco with William S. Burroughs. Its inclusion in the book was allegedly accidental and a joke, but it caused a sensation. In the book Toklas describes it as "the food of paradise" and hints at where one might score some weed, but like any sensible sinsemilla chef, warns that two pieces are enough to induce hysterical fits of laughter and wild floods of thoughts on "many simultaneous planes." Her infamy was sealed with the title of the 1968 Peter Sellers' film, *I Love You Alice B. Toklas*, which used hash brownies as a major plot device.

PERSONAL ANECDOTE:
──── ORDERING FROM THE MENU ────

I GOT MY FIRST MEDICAL MARIJUANA prescription in 2006, when things in California were more like the Montana Land Grab with a garnish of Wild, Wild West. I actually had no idea that L.A. had already "gone green," until I'd seen an early episode of *Weeds* in which Doug gets a 'script, prompting Nancy to sort of tour the clubs in The Valley. "Could it be that easy?" I thought. Short answer: yup.

The examination by a doctor back then averaged about $200—it's about $40 now—which I was happy to pay, because at the time, I was probably paying more in gas driving 60 miles to Riverside to buy it from my college roommate. Also, the examinations then were like getting a smog check for your car—it was "pass or don't pay." It went something like this:

DOCTOR: So what brings you in here today?
ME: Insomnia.
DOCTOR: How long have you been smoking marijuana to deal with that?
ME: About 15 years.
DOCTOR: Does it work?
ME: Yes.

And BOOM! The heavens parted and I had my medical marijuana card! (Which is a bit of a scam because you get a paper prescription too, and no collective/shop will take the card alone.)

I was provided with a list of legal collectives, and about a half hour later I was in line, as if ordering in a sandwich shop. Above all else, I remember being overwhelmed by the sheer number of strains on the menu board. And just when I thought things couldn't get more surreal, an actor from *Twin Peaks* got in line behind me. In the immortal words of Randy Newman, "I love L.A.!"

"Dope will get you through times of no money better than money will get you through times of no dope."
GILBERT SHELTON *Freewheelin' Franklin in*
The Fabulous Furry Freak Brothers *(1972)*

ETYMOLOGY: TOKE (VERB)

Inhaling a small amount marijuana cigarette or pipe smoke. US slang (circa 1952), possibly derived from the Spanish word, *tocar,* meaning "touch, tap, hit" or "get a shave or part."

HEMP FOR VICTORY

THIS US PUBLIC INFORMATION FILM was made in 1942 at a time when resources were low due to the Second World War. It actively encouraged farmers to grow industrial hemp as a means of producing rope, paper, and canvas. After the war the film was forgotten about (or suppressed, if you're a conspiracy fan) until 1989, when activists Jack Herer, Maria Farrow, and Carl Packard finally managed to uncover a recording of it on some old VHS tapes and donated them to the Library of Congress. This wasn't the first time US farmers were encouraged to grow hemp (400,000lbs of seeds were distributed). The first president of the USA, George Washington, grew it and famously wrote, "Make the most you can of the Indian Hemp seed and sow it everywhere." *Popular Mechanics* ran an article in February, 1938 entitled, *New Billion Dollar Crop,* stating, "…The connection of hemp as a crop and marijuana seems to be exaggerated. The drug is usually produced from wild hemp or locoweed, which can be found on vacant lots and along railroad tracks in every state. If federal regulations can be drawn to protect the public without preventing the legitimate culture of hemp, this vast new crop can add immeasurably to American agriculture and industry." Obviously, they couldn't. *Hemp for Victory* was eventually adapted into a 1993 underground comic by Art Penn.

Plate 28   Preparing Hemp II

Vol. I, Oeconomie rustique, Culture et Travail du Chanvre, Pl. II.

——SUBURBAN SINSEMILLA PRODUCTION——

IT'S ESTIMATED THAT ALMOST 50 PERCENT of all cannabis in the United Kingdom is home grown in "factories" or "farms." These are often in unassuming suburban houses that have had six months' rent paid as cash in advance. On moving day, all the furnishings are typically stripped out and vast hydroponic weed beds are installed. The amount of strong lighting and irrigation required for indoor growth generates huge and noticeable levels of thermal radiation (heat), which gives them away to police using thermal-imaging cameras. Another clue that's a red flag is an excessive electricity bill, which can be well over £300 ($480) per month. Many growers bypass this by tapping directly into the electricity supply, with the added danger of house fires. In 2006, in London alone, 50 farms were discovered this way.

Unfortunately, many South East Asian—particularly Vietnamese— gangs set these up and use illegal immigrant child labor to manage their farms. So make sure your supply is ethically sourced! Gangs often grow a single crop for three months and then move to another property, keeping one step ahead of the narcs and leaving the landlords with a devastated property. As one home grower, "Jimmy," explained to the BBC in 2008, "It's a big shame that the organized gangs are taking over. They don't believe in cannabis—to them it's just a way to make money."

Despite all these risks, it's still cheaper and safer for wholesale growers to produce the home-grown stuff rather than trying to smuggle cannabis into the country from abroad.

IDEAL WEED ON TV

SMOKIN' AND TOKIN' POPS UP all the time in TV shows, from *Shameless* to *Mad Men*, but there have been two outstanding series that have focused exclusively on dope dealers, both of which ran for almost the same length of time. In *Weeds* (2005–2012), Nancy Botwin (played by Mary-Louise Parker) is a widowed Californian suburban housewife who turns to dealing grass to cope financially after her husband's sudden death leaves her family on the brink of bankruptcy. The show follows Nancy's journey from setting up a dealership, finding a client base, and eventually moving on to grow her own supply, and creating her own strain of weed called MILF (slang abbreviation for Mom I'd Like to F**k)! Despite the potentially controversial subject matter, the show was a critical and commercial success, winning a Golden Globe and two Emmys.

In the UK, Graham Duff's darkly surreal sitcom, *Ideal* (get it?) starred Johnny Vegas as Moz, an agoraphobic weed merchant, and focused on the bizarre clients that popped by his Salford flat to score a lid. Running from 2005 until 2011, the storylines featured everything from necrophilia and deadly hit men to killer triads and a character with a mouse mask superglued to his face, known only as "Cartoon Head." Duff explained, "Moz isn't a big player in the world of drugs—far from it. Despite his profession, he actually has principles and won't deal in anything other than cannabis…As a hash dealer, Moz only sees snatches of people's lives—the bits they choose to parade in front of him—but he doesn't see the truth of these people." Duff continued, "The drugs are just a dramatic device. *Ideal* isn't about drugs, it's about the people who have this one thing in common and how their lives interact due to their shared need." Indeed, Moz sees himself as "providing a crucial service to the community." Throughout series five and six Moz gives up dealing, but he eventually returns to selling grass by the final series.

Both TV shows hit a particular zeitgeist, and while both were very dark comedy/dramas, each had a particular idiosyncratic feel relevant to their settings.

CHARAS: A JOINT OPERATION

THIS 2004 BOLLYWOOD ACTION FLICK had British Asian, Dev Anand (Jimmy Shergill) teaming up with an undercover Indian cop (Uday Chopra) to bust marijuana and opium drug barons in the infamous growing valleys of the Ladakh region of India. The convoluted plot twists and turns as Dev searches for his missing botanist pal, Sam, and it is a pretty good film if you can get over the obligatory song and dance numbers.

─── ETYMOLOGY: BLUNT (NOUN) ───

This is street slang for "marijuana and tobacco cigar," which started being used in the US around 1993, but is thought to have originated as early as the eighties among Jamaicans in New York City. The term is based on the Phillies Blunt brand cigars, which produce a sweeter smoke. The leaf wrapper of a Phillies Blunt is strong enough to hold together through the process of making a blunt, which involves cutting open and removing the cigar's interior and filling it with weed. However, these days it's much simpler to buy cognac- and honey-dipped tobacco leaves, ready for rolling a nice fat blunt. Can also be used as an adjective—"I got blunted" as in stoned or wasted.

"They've outlawed the number one vegetable on the planet."
TIMOTHY LEARY, *Psychologist and Writer (1920-1996)*

─── HANDY HEMP ───

POSSIBLY THE MOST VERSATILE PLANT crop on the planet, hemp has over 50,000 different uses. In the 1800s, and earlier, hemp was one of the most prolific crops used in the industrial manufacture of rope and ships' canvas sails and was a common livestock feed. Even vintage Levi's jeans were made with 40 percent hemp fiber. These days industrial hemp is grown on over 600,000 acres around the world—from Germany and Romania to China—and is used to make beer, flour, cooking oil, and numerous non-intoxicating foods. It makes excellent clothing, soaps, shampoos, sunblock, skateboards, housing materials, and paper products. It has even been extruded into a biodegradable plastic to make bags and CD cases. The Hemp Industries Association (HIA) was established in 1992 to promote and campaign for the fair and equal treatment of hemp in commercial use in North America.

"The mo' dedicated the mo' medicated."
SNOOP DOGG, *Musician (b. 1971)*

HEROES OF HEMP: JOE ROGAN

JOE ROGAN IS ONE OF THOSE annoying people who can do pretty much anything. He's an actor, a martial artist, a comedian, a writer, a producer, a television host, and a sports commentator. Suffice it to say, this guy gets around. But what we're most concerned with here are his activities as a marijuana user and legalization activist.

This Tae Kwon Do champion and Jiu-Jitsu black belt has been a very vocal champion of the positive effects and benefits of smoking weed for years, both from medical and spiritual standpoints. Though he didn't start properly smoking until he was around thirty (he started late because he bought into the hype that it's a gateway drug and will make you stupid like so many of us), he mostly views marijuana as a spiritual aid, something to clear his head, increase focus and concentration, and help him get in touch with himself. He's also stated that he's found success using it as a workout tool, which, considering how much of a pain fitness can be, is no surprise.

But Rogan does more than just smoke weed, he also evangelizes it. He starred in the 2007 documentary, *The Union: The Business Behind Getting High*, about marijuana prohibition, which likens the war on drugs in this instance to alcohol prohibition in the 1920s, complete with attendant rises in organized crime and lengthy sentences for simple personal possession. Rogan also presented the History Channel documentary *Marijuana: A Chronic History* and has appeared on Marijuana Marketing TV on YouTube. Rogan will often take weed's detractors head on in an erudite debate, blinding them with science and anecdotes of his own personal (positive) experiences with the drug—one of his finest moments was verbally bitch-slapping Dr. Drew for spreading the ridiculous notion that marijuana is addictive and a gateway drug to bath salts (?!). For his tireless advocacy on behalf of our herbal friend, and his ability to talk twice as fast as a normal human, Joe Rogan takes a trophy.

> "Our federal government prohibited this organic plant based on lies, continues to classify it among the most dangerous drugs to validate billions in funding pointless agendas, and denies its medical value, causing countless lives to suffer needlessly. How can anyone not care?"
>
> ROB VAN DAM, *American Pro Wrestler (active 1990–Present)*

—— CANNABUTTER ——

THERE'S MORE TO COOKING with weed than just chucking a bunch of leaves and buds into a pot and stirring. If you really want to get that buzz you've got to release the active ingredient, Tetrahydrocannabinol (THC), from the plant. Because THC isn't water soluble, you need to break it down in fats or oil and the best way to do this is to make cannabutter or ghee. Here's how to make the former:

1 You'll need 1–2lbs (0.5–1kg) of butter and 2–3oz (55–85g) of finely ground/powdered marijuana tops or buds. This should make more than enough for several recipes.

2 Melt the butter on a low heat and then add the grass. Simmer slowly until the butter turns a greenish color. Be careful not to burn the butter as that will ruin the flavor and destroy the THC. "Slow and low" is best.

3 Next, strain the butter through a very fine sieve or muslin and set the leafy material aside.

4 If you really want to up the potency of the butter you can repeat steps 1–3 with a bunch of fresh marijuana, but go easy, cannabis in cooking takes twice as long as a joint to cause a high, but it is twice as strong! So always err on the side of caution.

5 When the cannabutter has cooled you can refrigerate or freeze and use as needed. It's a good idea to pour a little water over the top, which seals it for freshness.

6 The leftover leafy material can be simmered in hot milk and sweetened with honey to make a delicious dope drink. Just remember to take it easy!

HERB VS. "HERB"

THE RELATIONSHIP BETWEEN marijuana and dried oregano is as long as it is contentious. There are many documented (and tragic) cases of unscrupulous dealers selling innocuous old oregano to newbies in the guise of weed. What's more, there's also no shortage of anecdotes of those same amateurs later smoking their top-quality oregano and either pretending or believing they're toking the real reefer (belief is a powerful thing). The confusion is understandable to a point; while the two dried plants share the same dirty green hue and do look similar from a distance (dealers will often wrap the fake weed up well in semi-transparent plastic), the real divider is the smell. If your herb smells like it belongs in an Italian restaurant, don't try to smoke it. If it has a top-note of skunk (the animal—hence the variety name), you're probably in possession of the real thing. It's perfectly acceptable to take a whiff of the product before making a purchase, and at the end of the day, practice makes perfect.

(On a related note, tomato plants are sometimes mistaken for pot plants, so be sure to keep interfering neighbors away from your legal vegetable garden.)

> "The only effect that I ever noticed from smoking marijuana was a sort of mild sedative, a release of tension when I was overworking."
>
> ROBERT MITCHUM, *Actor (1917–1997)*

TOP 15 DOPEST HIP-HOP TUNES

These rappers are all about the chronic:

1 *HIGH ALL TIME* BY 50 CENT (*Get Rich or Die Tryin'*, 2003)

2 *GET HIGH TONIGHT* BY BUSTA RHYMES (*When Disaster Strikes*, 1997)

3 *PACK THE PIPE* BY THE PHARCYDE (*Bizarre Ride II the Pharcyde*, 1992)

4 *INDO SMOKE* BY MISTER GRIMM (*Poetic Justice Soundtrack*, 1983)

5 *TICAL* BY METHOD MAN (*Tical*, 1994)

6 *HOW HIGH* BY REDMAN AND METHOD MAN (*The Blackout*, 1999)

7 *I CAN'T WAKE UP* BY KRS-ONE (*Return of the Boom Bap*, 1993)

8 *HOW TO ROLL A BLUNT* BY REDMAN (*Whut? Thee Album*, 1992)

9 *DOOBIE ASHTRAY* BY DEVIN THE DUDE (*Just Tryin' ta Live*, 2002)

10 *WEED SONG* BY BONE THUGS-N-HARMONY (*BTNHresurrection*, 2000)

11 *I WANNA GET HIGH* BY CYPRESS HILL (*Black Sunday*, 1993)

12 *CHEEBA CHEEBA* BY TONE LOC (*Loc-ed After Dark*, 1989)

13 *SMOKE SOME WEED* BY ICE CUBE (*Laugh Now, Cry Later*, 2006)

14 *DOWN 2 THA LAST ROACH* BY EAZY-E (*It's On (Dr. Dre) 187um Killa*, 1993)

15 *THE ROACH* BY DR. DRE (*The Chronic*, 1992)

A MOMENT OF SILENCE
FOR THE LESS FORTUNATE

ONE COULD BE FORGIVEN FOR ASSUMING this book has come down on the pro-marijuana side of the great pot debate, mostly because it has. We've discussed the medicinal value of pot, both scientifically proved and anecdotally suggested; the value of hemp to industry and environment; reasons for its prohibition; reasons for and against medical and general legalization; how to roll a joint; recipes; and basically just how fun the stuff is…for most people. But weed has a little-discussed dark side that even its most determined advocates cannot deny.

Cannabis is a drug, but first and foremost, it's a plant. More specifically, it's a flowering herb. Despite marijuana's medical benefits, between ten and 30 percent of the world's population may be excluded from using this wondrous drug because of a single side effect: allergies. That's right: standard, run-of-the-mill, summer-is-hell-kill-me-now-oh-god pollen and plant allergies.

While marijuana allergies haven't been investigated in depth, some people have reported skin rashes, hives, rhinitis, flu-like symptoms, and breathing problems after indulging. This is hardly surprising given the plant connection and experts believe that marijuana allergies might be more common than previously assumed. In 2011, Dr. Gordon Sussman, acting division director of clinical allergy and immunology at the University of Toronto, conducted a study of 17 patients who complained of allergic reactions following cannabis use and all 17 tested positive for sensitivity following skin-prick tests. One patient experienced anaphylactic shock from drinking marijuana tea. The causes and mechanics of the allergies aren't well known and probably won't be any time soon; it's difficult to conduct proper studies on illegal drugs, even in clinical and academic environments, and marijuana allergies are most likely drastically under reported because patients are (understandably) reluctant to confess illegal drug use to their doctors.

Do not condemn these unfortunate individuals, fair reader; do not laugh or jeer at this profound disability. Instead, treat them as they deserve to be treated—with pity. They deserve our sympathy and compassion.

—————————— HIP-HOP HEMPSTERS ——————————

THIS CATEGORY OF SMOKER is densely populated. Not only is marijuana use and reference rife in hip-hop culture, it's at the level of being almost a badge of honor. These are some of our favorite musical icons who also happen to be massive stoners.

1 METHOD MAN AND REDMAN

Rap's finest comedy duo has what could accurately be called prolific smoking habits and they aren't afraid to tweet the visual evidence. Their music, both as solo artists and a team, is filled with references to their favorite pastime— witness *How High*, *A Special Joint*, and *Dis Iz 4 All My Smokers* among many, many others—and they even starred in their own ill-reviewed but cult favorite stoner film *How High* (2001). We want them to be our best friends.

2 CYPRESS HILL

With titles like *I Love You Mary Jane*, *Roll It Up, Light It Up, Smoke It Up*, and *K.U.S.H.*, most Cypress Hill tracks read like love letters to weed, and their songs regularly appear on lists of the best songs to get high by. Their rep is further fueled by the fact that they have an uncanny ability to sound like smoking feels.

3 SNOOP DOGG

Snoop Dogg is the incarnate existence of herbal celebration. He smokes it, he loves it, he lives it. The music connections are obvious, but he often shows up as the pimping and/or pot-loving minor character when needed in movies and TV shows. We even liked his horror anthology movie *Hood of Horror* (2002) just because he was in it, even though it really wasn't very good and isn't the kind of thing you want to watch while smoking.

4 CURREN$Y

Smoking weed isn't just something this New Orleans native does; it's an integral part of his whole public (and we're betting private) identity. All of the references in his music are there, but he's also an outspoken smoker outside of his lyrics. He's also been known to give advice to fellow enthusiasts; according to Curren$y, blunts are expensive and bad for you, so stick to papers.

5 WIZ KHALIFA

This man isn't just a weed smoker, he's a *connoisseur*. This man has his own strain of marijuana, Khalifa Kush, which was cultivated for him according to his taste and personal high preferences. But don't go looking for it at your medical dispensary or (legal) recreational shop just yet—it's still too rare for general consumption.

POTUMENTARIES

A MIDST THE MANY SILLY-ASS fiction movies that revolve around smoking-related high jinx and the anti-marijuana propaganda films masquerading as nonfiction, there are some pretty informative films on the market for anyone looking for less negative and/or more scientific views of the herb. Here are five documentaries we recommend for education rather than entertainment (some of which are available in their entirety on YouTube):

1 IN POT WE TRUST (2007) This pro-pot film takes a look at legalization in the US and features arguments from both sides of the aisle. Through interviews with academics, politicians, and political lobbyists, the police, DEA officials, and medical marijuana users (including those specifically supplied by the federal government—that's right: *federal*, not state), *In Pot We Trust* intersperses personal stories of those who've been helped by marijuana for medical use. If you're already pro-legalization for medical use, it'll be preaching to the converted, but those on the fence or in the anti camp may have their eyes opened a little to pot's benefits for those who suffer.

2 THE UNION: THE BUSINESS BEHIND GETTING HIGH (2007) Featuring the well known Hero of Hemp, Joe Rogen, *The Union* is staunchly and unabashedly pro-legalization and it makes an excellent case. Through a brief history lesson, comparisons to alcohol prohibition, and expert and enthusiast interviews, the film attempts to prove that the war on drugs began as a war on marijuana in the 1970s, intended to stamp out political unrest, specifically Vietnam War protests. The resultant anti-drug machine has become such big business with so many tentacles that it's in the government's (and many private sectors') best interest to keep marijuana illegal. It's a fairly depressing outlook on the legalization of weed in the US, but an essential educational tool.

3 GRASS: THE HISTORY OF MARIJUANA (1999) Narrated by noted pothead Woody Harrelson, *Grass* chronicles the troubled history of marijuana in the USA, starting with its link to Mexican laborers and progressing through to Anslinger's involvement and decades of government anti-drug propaganda. The film is more colorful and lighthearted than the other docs on this list, but its message is still clear: The US government's marijuana policy is misguided and harmful to the American public.

4 SUPER HIGH ME (2007) Comedian and pothead Doug Benson takes the Morgan Spurlock challenge, but with marijuana: he spends 30 days not smoking at all, followed by 30 days of smoking all day, every day. Benson takes physical and mental tests both while smoking and sober, for comparison, and the results are surprising, if not groundbreaking. Benson's story is peppered with the processes and plights of medical dispensaries in California, and includes an interview with Hero of Hemp Marc Emery.

5 MARIJUANA INC.: INSIDE AMERICA'S POT INDUSTRY (2009) Produced by CNBC, this doc investigates the pot industry in northern California, from legal growing to smuggling, and its effects on the local culture and economy. It's remarkably evenhanded for having been produced by one of the major US news networks, but highlights the difficulty and consequences of growing in a legal state where federal laws still outlaw cultivation and consumption.

THE BIG APPLE BONG

EARLY IN 2014, New York State governor Andrew Cuomo announced he would allow limited use of marijuana for medical reasons (marijuana had previously been illegal for all uses). On the one hand, we wonder what took so long for such a purportedly liberal state that includes New York City, that bastion of excess and hedonism, among its constituents to get on the weed bandwagon. On the other hand, Cuomo has historically opposed medical marijuana, New York State still has the death penalty, and NYC has proved enough of a nanny city to ban e-cigarettes in public and require all chain restaurants to post calorie counts (because otherwise we'd think McDonald's is serving up the elixir of life blended into a McFlurry).

But don't go planning your move to the Big Apple yet—medical marijuana in New York will be tightly controlled and restricted for use only in a handful of hospitals and by the seriously ill, so insomnia and occasional tension headaches won't get you a weed card like those California hippies. But don't despair: in a larger sense, New York is now the twenty-first state in the US to legalize medical marijuana, which is just another step toward universal acceptance.

"Look, when I was a kid, I inhaled. Frequently. That was the point."

BARACK OBAMA, *US President (b. 1961)*

POT PENS

C ANNABIS VAPORIZERS HAVE BEEN on the market for ages, but they've always been relatively expensive and unwieldy. Classic, cone-shaped vaporizers can run to hundreds of dollars, but many smokers prefer them as they provide a healthier alternative to lighting the weed on fire and dragging the particulates into their lungs. Used with either buds or oil, vaporizers give a stronger high with less damage to both the source material and the smoker. But they've never been a particularly portable alternative to smoking, and this is where e-cigarettes have come in to lend a bit of technological innovation to their less-legal brother.

Like traditional cigarettes, e-cigarettes were designed to be carried around and puffed at will, aping the "oh my god I need something to do with my hands and what about my oral fixation" habit of the daily smoker (one of the many reasons that patches, inhalers, and cold-turkey quitting fail so often—they don't satisfy the *act* of smoking, just the nicotine addiction). So lo and behold the e-cigarette was born and it's amazing. The device, in its most basic sense, works by heating up a mixture of liquid nicotine and a carrier agent (often propylene glycol) to create a vapor that can be inhaled. It wasn't long before some intrepid young potheads noticed that the e-cigarette device could be applied to "smoking"—properly termed vaping—hash oil as well. The original technology needed to be modified as you can't just pour some oil into a standard e-cigarette and achieve the desired results—although there are hacks available—but there are now pens on the market that look and act very much like e-cigarettes and can be used with oils, waxes, and dry herb. Of course, this stealth ability just may be their undoing, as twitchy lawmakers are starting to realize that, in public, it's hard to tell the difference between someone legally vaping nicotine and illegally vaping cannabis. Only time will tell whether this new technology will be "regulated" into oblivion by the THINK OF THE CHILDREN! brigade, so there may be only a limited time in which to buy devices to vape the reefer. Go forth and conquer.

——— HEROES OF HEMP: MARC EMERY ———

POPULARLY KNOWN AS "The Prince of Pot," Marc Emery has shown his activist chops in a variety of ways, from leading a legalization-platform political party to supplying paraphernalia and seeds to the people. This guy has done just about everything he can in the name of weed.

Originally from London, Ontario in Canada, Emery demonstrated an entrepreneurial spirit early on by forming mail-order businesses before he even went through puberty. If that doesn't make you feel inadequate enough, he bought and ran a bookshop while he was still a teenager, and then started to participate seriously in local politics in his early twenties. He clearly had a problem with government censorship and "nanny state" intervention, as he would sell banned albums and literature (including *High Times* magazine) specifically to contravene Canadian law.

After moving to Vancouver in the mid-nineties, Emery opened a head shop, which was a bit of a problem as it was illegal to sell drug paraphernalia and literature in Canada at the time. At this point, he'd more than proved his willingness to break laws he didn't agree with, which makes him sound like a bit of a jerk, but his end game was nobler than it seemed. Emery soon sponsored a case against Canada's laws prohibiting the sale of paraphernalia and literature, and he succeeded in overturning the prohibition. A year later Emery started a marijuana mag of his own: *Cannabis Culture*.

However, Emery's head for business and law-breaking eventually became his downfall. His head shop also sold seeds, and after numerous raids and fines, he switched to mail-order only in the late nineties. As he would ship anywhere in the world, his distribution efforts became an international issue, and in 2005 he was arrested at the request of the US Drug Enforcement Agency for international drug trafficking. Amidst worldwide protests, Emery spent the next five years fighting extradition to the US. He eventually copped a plea and was sentenced to five years in US federal prison.

Marc Emery is one of the most important Heroes of Hemp to emerge out of the past thirty years, because he didn't just use cannabis, talk about how great it is, or make money off it; he also helped bring the legalization issue to worldwide political attention and actually changed the arcane anti-cannabis laws in Canada. Despite raids, fines, arrests, harassment, and ultimately imprisonment, he's remained a staunchly vocal and political supporter of smokers' rights and a hero to decriminalization and legalization movements globally. It's probably a bit of an overstatement to say he's the Gandhi of weed, but Emery has certainly been the change he wished to see in the world.

PAPERS TO READ, NOT ROLL

APPARENTLY POTHEADS LIKE TO READ. A lot. So it's a good thing there are so many sources of information in print and online, giving everything from reviews to advice to techniques and interviews. These are four of the more established magazines available to the discerning weed aficionado today:

1 HIGH TIMES: No discussion of marijuana-reading material can be considered complete without mentioning *High Times*. First published in 1974, the magazine has become the *Playboy* of pot, complete with a monthly fold-out centerfold (but most people read it for the articles). Willing to change with the times, *High Times* is now available online as well as in print, and in 2010 launched *Medical Marijuana News & Reviews*, a sister publication devoted to medical marijuana activism.

2 CANNABIS CULTURE: Launched in 1995 under the name *Cannabis Canada*, *Cannabis Culture* was founded by Marc Emery, a noted legalization activist, who became the leader of the British Columbia Marijuana Party in 2000. The publication dropped print and became wholly online in 2005, where it provides readers with news and views on the struggle of legalization, as well as growing tips and interviews with cannacelebrities.

3 420 MAGAZINE: This California-based magazine is the largest publication in the US based on the medical marijuana movement and has been preaching to readers since 1993. Its mission is to support the full legalization of cannabis throughout the world, and it does that by educating its readers with facts, news, scientific data, legal information, and an online community forum for like-minded people.

4 CANNABIS NOW: One of the newer magazines on this list, *Cannabis Now* is devoted almost entirely to the medical marijuana movement. Its prime objective is education, and as such, it's less about celebrity interviews and more dedicated to pieces on responsible consumption; political, economic, and legal news and commentary; and researched-based facts and figures on the drug to combat the hysteria and ignorance that largely prevent legalization.

THE CANNABIS CONSPIRACY

IN THE COMICS WORLD, British artist and writer Bryan Talbot is no joke. He began his career in comics with underground comix in the sixties and progressed to *The Adventures of Luther Arkwright* in the late seventies, the comic series for which he is probably most famous. That was still the beginning of his career, however, and since then he's worked on *Judge Dredd* for 2000 AD, *Sandman* and *Batman* for DC Comics, and *Fables* for Vertigo. His own creations include *Alice in Sunderland*, *Grandville*, *The Tale of One Bad Rat*, and, most relevant to this book, *The Cannabis Conspiracy*.

The Cannabis Conspiracy is only four pages long, but the Eagle and Eisner Award-winning creator packs in quite a bit. Beginning with a short history of marijuana and hemp in America, Talbot posits that the prohibition of cannabis began as a conspiracy orchestrated by William Randolph Hearst, the Dupont family, and Andrew Mellon to ban hemp in favor of their own profitable and patented methods of paper, rope, and cloth manufacture. It all seems a bit hysterical at first—a paranoid fantasy invented by a sixties flower child—but taking a step back, it does make a sick kind of sense. Approaching the marijuana debate from whatever angle you like, it will eventually be distilled down to a matter of money—whether it's the money that flows through the government anti-drug machine, the lack of profit for pharmaceutical companies that have tried and failed for decades to produce an effective synthetic version in light of the fact that plants can't be patented, or the campaign dollars politicians won't receive if they endorse marijuana legalization in their conservative districts. And this doesn't even begin to address the industries that depend on deforestation for their products, and which would probably go out of business if hemp became a legal alternative for creating paper and other saleable fibers.

In light of the current political and financial climate in the US, is it really that farfetched to suggest that cannabis prohibition began as a way for the richest and most powerful men in America to stay rich and powerful? Whether you believe it or not, *The Cannabis Conspiracy* will make you consider that question carefully, and when you're done, you might just need a little weed to lift the depression.

THAT '70S SHOW: MYSTERY SOLVED

REMEMBER THE CIRCLE? Where different combinations of characters would sit around a table and everyone's eyes would be red, they all seemed really chilled out while they chatted, and the air would be suspiciously smoky but you never actually saw what was going on? Turns out they were smoking weed. For real. We're surprised too.

A VAGUE HISTORY OF MEDICAL MARIJUANA

IT SEEMS ODD THAT THE MODERN mainstream public has been so opposed to cannabis for so long, even for medicinal purposes, when the drug has been used as a healing aid by all sections of society, including the most venerated, for the past 5,000 years (that we know of). Let's skip back through history, shall we, and discover what our elders—some may say "betters"—were using this leafy little wonder drug for. You might be surprised how modern their marijuana sensibilities were.

CIRCA 2700 BC: Chinese Emperor Shen Nung is considered the father of Chinese medicine and is said to have eaten hundreds of herbs to determine whether they had any medicinal properties. Legend has it that he discovered the healing properties of weed and used it to treat pretty much everything, from malaria to diarrhea to (unsurprisingly) vomiting.

2000 TO 1400 BC: In India, cannabis was not only used as a spiritual aid, but also as an Ayurvedic remedy to treat insomnia, stress, and indigestion. Later it was purported to be a cure for leprosy.

CIRCA 1770 BC TO 1100 BC: Judging by their medical texts, the Ancient Egyptians loved themselves some herb. They used hemp oil mixed with honey to treat inflammation and pre-menstrual symptoms, as well as crushed up seeds for colorectal issues.

500 BC TO FIRST CENTURY AD: Medical men of the Greek and Roman persuasion found cannabis quite useful for problems such as earache and nosebleeds, but also used it to (ahem) "dry up the seed" of adolescent boys and warned that excessive use could cause sexual dysfunction.

FIFTEENTH CENTURY: Muslim scholars were faced with a dilemma over marijuana—they recognized its medicinal value, but also its intoxicating qualities, and debated whether it should be treated akin to alcohol, which is expressly forbidden by the Koran. They eventually decided to differentiate between the two uses, allowing medical marijuana, but severely punishing recreational use.

NINETEENTH CENTURY: Marijuana wasn't widely used in the US and Europe until Irish doctor William O'Shaughnessy conducted his own research into cannabis' medical applications. He used it to treat pain and the often-fatal symptoms of cholera. In 1860, the Ohio State Medical Society held the first American conference on medical marijuana, and found it to be successful in treating gonorrhea and pain, among other afflictions.

TWENTIETH CENTURY: Despite worldwide legality issues, marijuana is strongly indicated in the treatment of chronic pain, side effects from chemotherapy, loss of appetite, and symptoms of AIDS, for example. While not recognized as a cure for any disease, it can greatly increase quality of life in the sick by alleviating symptoms and side effects.

—— HEROES OF HEMP: LESTER GRINSPOON ——

IF YOU WATCH SOME OF THE POTUMENTARIES listed in this book, you'll recognize Lester Grinspoon. If you're a proponent of medical marijuana, you should know who he is anyway.

Currently an associate professor of psychiatry, emeritus, at Harvard Medical School, Grinspoon saw his friends and contemporaries use marijuana quite a bit during the sixties and, as a doctor, decided to do a little research into this drug he'd heard, and believed, was so harmful. His extensive investigation covered all research available in the Harvard libraries, and he came to believe that marijuana wasn't dangerous at all, despite the hype. At the time he published a book on that lack of danger called *Marihuana Reconsidered* in 1971—which included a pro-pot essay by "Mr. X," also known as Carl Sagan— Grinspoon's teenage son had been suffering the effects of chemotherapy used to treat his leukemia. The worst of it was constant vomiting and lack of appetite. While Grinspoon couldn't endorse his son's use of illegal drugs, his wife procured a little pot for their son to smoke, hoping to alleviate the chemo's side effects. Grinspoon then witnessed first-hand the medical benefits of weed, as his son stopped vomiting and regained his appetite. Though his son didn't make it in the end, Grinspoon believes that the quality of his remaining life was greatly increased by marijuana.

Since then, Grinspoon has wholeheartedly endorsed marijuana's medical applications, prompting scientific studies into its effectiveness as well as personally publishing on its ability to alleviate suffering in those afflicted with numerous diseases. Even though he believes his course of study may have affected the progress of his career, he has remained a vocal and important proponent of the drug, calling for its legalization as a medicine.

> "Marijuana will be legal some day, because the many law students who now smoke pot will someday become Congressmen and legalize it in order to protect themselves."
>
> LENNY BRUCE, *American comedian* (1925–1966)

STONER GAMES

ALTHOUGH BOARD GAMES SEEM to be a thing of the past these days, having been eclipsed by more recent entertainment inventions that beep and blink, and change images every half second, stoners still embrace the cards and dice. Probably because video games move just a bit too fast when you're high. Here are five board and card games that center around bud:

1 REEFER CITY: Billed as "the game for intelligent heads," Reefer City uses the standard Monopoly format with board, dice, cards, and funny money. The object is to make your way through the city selling weed, hash, and shrooms without getting arrested. It bundles entertainment and useful life skills into one box.

2 STONER CITY: Despite the similar title, this one is less imaginative than Reefer City. It's a straight Monopoly rip-off, with the only addition to gameplay being a police car that travels in the opposite direction of the players—when the car and a player land on the same space, the player goes to rehab (Stoner City's highly original version of jail).

3 STONER FLUXX: Fluxx is almost impossible to play drunk due to the complexity of its rules, so we're not sure how successful it would be to play the stoner version. The rules are basically the same, but with pot-themed cards, you can feel as good about the purchase as the play, because five percent of proceeds go to the Marijuana Policy Project, NORML, and other organizations devoted to legalizing marijuana.

4 THE OFFICIAL DEALER MCDOPE DEALING GAME: This game is no longer made, but it was a classic of the 1970s (and you can find it on any auction site or at garage sales). Created by legendary comix artist Dave Sheridan, Dealer McDope involves players buying and selling weed while avoiding prison. The first dealer to reach two million dollars wins. It's a lot to pack in to a board, dice, and a deck of cards.

5 TRAFFICKING: Originally created in the fabulous eighties, Trafficking has its players take on the roles of drug dealers and a Narc. The winner, or "Traffic King," is the first dealer to sell one kilo of marijuana without being arrested by the Narc. Controversial enough to be banned only a few years after it was released, Trafficking is now on the market again and will probably teach you more about business than any Ivy League school.

NORML

Founded in 1970 by attorney Keith Stroup, the National Organization for the Reform of Marijuana Laws (NORML) is dedicated to the decriminalization of marijuana. It has hundreds of chapters across the United States, as well as partner programs in other countries such as New Zealand, Ireland, and the United Kingdom). The organization also seeks to educate the public on marijuana, contradicting much of the false information disseminated by the government to support the War on Drugs by publishing detailed scholarly work on the subject of marijuana's medicinal use. They maintain an impressive media presence in a variety of venues, from billboards in Times Square, to television commercials, to petitions to the White House. They also use legal tools to keep the pressure on the government—in 1972 NORML sued the Drug Enforcement Administration, arguing for the legalization of medical marijuana. You'll also find their support and grassroots activist groups behind many state's individual decriminalization/legalization legislative pushes. Marijuana has now been decriminalized in some states and legalized in Washington and Colorado, but NORML still has a lot of work to do to achieve its goal of total acceptance. Luckily, it has the help of a star roster of an advisory board, which includes Willie Nelson, Woody Harrelson, Tommy Chong, Bill Maher, Nadine Strossen (president of the ACLU), and, formerly, Robert Altman and Hunter S. Thompson.

—— URUGUAY CROSSES THE FINISH LINE ——

José Mujica, the president of Uruguay, is known to be one of the most liberal politicians on the planet and rivals Pope Francis in the humility and charity departments. He gives about 90 percent of his salary to charity, lives on a farm instead of in the presidential palace, and drives a 25-year-old Volkswagen Beetle. In which case, it really shouldn't have been a surprise when this bleeding-heart hippie legalized marijuana in 2013.

Smoking has been legal in the country for decades, so Uruguay has gone a step further with its new legislation: the state is intent on fully creating, licensing, and regulating a countrywide marijuana industry. Once the law is put into effect, any registered adult will be able to grow weed in their own home, take part in a club to grow as a collective, or buy joints from pharmacies. By bringing control of the drug into state hands, Uruguayan law-makers hope to discourage the illegal drug trade, effectively stripping the cartels of their money and power.

Sounds like a pretty great idea, doesn't it? But the move isn't without its detractors (of course). The United Nations in particular has publicly denounced Uruguay's planned legalization, saying that it could hurt the country's children and contribute to addiction. Apparently the UN hasn't got the memo about cannabis not being a) addictive and b) a gateway drug. But then they probably still use *Reefer Madness* as a documentary/training video.

As much as Uruguay's new law may bode well for legalization, or at least decriminalization, on the international scene in the (distant?) future, and as much as we admire José Mujica's common-sense approach to the War on Drugs despite his personal dislike for recreational chemicals, don't go changing your holiday plans from Amsterdam to Uruguay just yet. The laws are also specifically designed to prevent marijuana tourism, as only registered adults will be able to buy the goods, and only citizens of Uruguay may register. There's no indication whether this will change anytime soon, so for now a weekend getaway to Denver might be in order (out-of-staters can legally buy a quarter of an ounce).

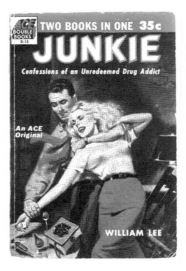

——— STONER GAMES 2: THE GAMENING ———

FOR THOSE OF YOU WHO LIKE your gaming action a bit more interactive—more "real," one might say—there are a few video games out there that feature the drug in creative ways. Here are four of the more direct references and one upcoming game that's more of an instructional video:

1 GRAND THEFT AUTO SERIES: Weed has been a minor staple of the *GTA* franchise since the beginning, with many characters indulging in a bit of herb here and there (the main character never smokes himself, but he does deal and run drug missions for others). In *San Andreas*, an entire mission involves burning a weed field for an old hippie voiced by none other than Peter Fonda, which is quite the tribute.

2 AFRO SAMURAI: Originally a manga series that was then adapted to anime, Afro Samurai is, unsurprisingly, a black samurai hell bent on revenge. Although the suspiciously cone-shaped roll-up perpetually hanging out of his mouth isn't explicitly referred to as a joint, have a look and draw your own conclusion. (Bonus evidence: Afro is voiced by Samuel L. Jackson.)

3 SAINTS ROW 1 AND 2: *Saints Row* takes the *GTA* casual weed use a bit further by allowing the main character to buy and smoke, but also suffer its effects. While we wouldn't normally equate smoking with suffering, the character control takes a hit from distorted vision and coughing fits.

4 CALL OF JUAREZ: THE CARTEL: Seeing as this is a game based on Mexican drug cartels, it's of no surprise that marijuana should make a prominent showing. The somewhat depressing gameplay involves a shoot out in a marijuana field, and no one gets high. Not much fun, then.

5 GROWSIM: At the end of 2013, creator Matt Di Spirito released the Beta version of his indie *GROWsim* "game," which is basically a simulation of how to grow medical marijuana. This doesn't really fit into the entertainment category, but it certainly has educational value, so it may be the most justifiable game on this list to spend money on.

"Never smoke pot before there's a possibility of talking to a hundred million people."

WHOOPI GOLDBERG, *Actress (b. 1955)*

——— WRITING UNDER THE INFLUENCE ———

A UTHORIAL TYPES HAVE NEVER BEEN strangers to drugs—in fact, they have a bit of a reputation for enjoying the more hedonistic things in life. Some prefer booze, others LSD, but the creators on this list are prime examples of the benefits of writing while baked.

1 AARON SORKIN
It's not that hard to work out Sorkin's had problems with drugs, as every TV show he writes has at least one recovering-addict-turned-wiseman on the character roster. Autobiographical much? Anyway, his particular cocktail contains, among others, the reefer, which he apparently tokes (or toked) to get his creative juices flowing.

2 RICK STEVES
This one's a little unexpected, considering Steves' reputation for being popular with independent travelers of a certain age, but perhaps his soporific demeanor gave us the clue. Steves believes the drug's mind-expanding qualities have made him become a better writer (with more than 20 bestselling guidebooks on the market, he should know). But Steves goes beyond mere use, as he's also a strong advocate of decriminalization, evidenced by his seat on the board of directors of NORML. He also worked on the TV program *Marijuana: It's Time for a Conversation*, which was produced by the ACLU.

3 STEPHEN KING

King is another writer who's had drug problems in the past (let's not be too surprised—writing is a pain in the ass), and much of his work during the eighties doesn't bode well for writers who want to use cocaine as a creative stimulant. Weed, however, is a different story, and King is enough of a fan to advocate legalization.

4 LEE CHILD

In August 2013, Lee Child, the bestselling author of the Jack Reacher novels, told the *Daily Mail* newspaper that he's "been smoking weed for 44 years, five nights a week." Considering he's on his way to reaching 100 million in book sales, it doesn't seem to have done his writing career any harm and could even be considered an asset.

5 ALEXANDRE DUMAS AND FRIENDS

The author of *The Count of Monte Cristo*, *The Three Musketeers*, and many other stories of romance and adventure liked his hashish and no mistake. Along with Charles Baudelaire, Honoré de Balzac, and Victor Hugo, Dumas was a member of the Club des Hashischins, which was dedicated to exploring mind-altering experiences with drugs like opium and, more often, hashish. While Dumas is perhaps the most populist writer of the group, the one thing all these men have in common is that, more than 100 years after their deaths, they're still widely known and read. Not bad for a bunch of nineteenth-century stoners.

6 HUNTER S. THOMPSON

This entry on the list should be a surprise to exactly nobody, but it has to be said that among all the other drugs Thompson indulged in, marijuana was one of his favorites. He's called it "one of the staples of life," has served on the board of NORML, advocated legalization, and smoked right up to the end of his life because he believed the drug prevented Alzheimer's. And if recent research is anything to go by, he wasn't far off the mark.

7 CARL SAGAN

Astrophysicist, author, luminary, pothead. Carl Sagan not only smoked marijuana himself, he advocated its use for its mind-expanding properties, and even contributed an essay to *Marihuana Reconsidered*, published in 1971, using the pseudonym "Mr. X." He wrote that "the illegality of cannabis is outrageous, an impediment to full utilization of a drug which helps produce the serenity and insight, sensitivity and fellowship so desperately needed in this increasingly mad and dangerous world." While his advocacy and use was kept secret until after his death, he still managed to communicate his beliefs on the drug as effectively as those on science.

8 ALAN MOORE

The author of such groundbreaking comics as *Watchmen*, *V for Vendetta*, *From Hell*, and *Batman: The Killing Joke* is also a massive stoner. In between his duties worshipping Glycon, his snake god, and performing ceremonial magic, Moore smokes what has been termed a "prodigious" amount of weed. According to artist Rick Veitch, "Next time you read one of Alan's extensive interviews in print or online, and are marveling at the fact he is speaking off the cuff like Herman Melville wrote novels on a good day, you can probably be certain the interview was conducted under the influence of enough wacky tobbacky to put Cheech and Chong under the table."

9 WILLIAM BUTLER YEATS

Nobel Prize-winning poet Yeats was a keen believer in the occult, going so far as joining the Hermetic Order of the Golden Dawn and the Theosophical Society, both dedicated to mystic ritual and investigation. Of course, mind-expanding activities such as these are often aided by the use of mind-altering drugs, and Yeats began using hashish in pellet form in the 1890s after visiting Paris, that notorious hotbed of cannabactivity. He used the drug to enhance creativity and commune with mystical forces, and considering he won a Nobel, it seems to have worked.

10 ALLEN GINSBERG

Drugs and the Beat Generation go hand in hand. While Ginsberg and his contemporaries are most known for their use and advocacy of LSD, Ginsberg also supported marijuana legalization. In 1966 he published an essay in *The Atlantic Monthly* called "The Great Marijuana Hoax: First Manifesto to End the Bringdown," which chronicled his own use of the drug while making a case for the absurdity of its illegality. He also mentions that most of the creatives he knows—actors, musicians, writers, artists, poets, and sculptors—have been smoking for decades. Which is pretty much what we've been saying all along.

"Wine makes men happy and sociable; hashish isolates them. Wine exalts the will; hashish annihilates it."

CHARLES BAUDELAIRE, *Poet (1821–1867)*

—— EAR WAX: IT'LL BLOW YOUR ASS UP ——

EAR WAX is a relative newcomer to the hash scene. Named for its brown, sticky, ear waxy appearance, it's estimated to be anywhere from 50 to 90 percent THC (by contrast, the flower alone is more like five to ten percent). Seems like heaven, one might think, but it's already caused some trouble due to its method of manufacture and its effects.

It's easy to find tutorials on how to make Ear Wax on YouTube, but the most common method seems to be to soak the bud in butane to extract the oil (known as BHO, or butane hash oil), evaporate the butane, and then heat the oil to concentrate it into a thick, golden-brown resin. Seems relatively simple and straightforward, doesn't it? Unfortunately, when cannabis resin production starts to resemble cooking meth, (breaking) bad things are going to happen. So it was with two Brooklyn, New York, teenagers in 2013 who thought it would be a good idea to fill a barrel with butane and then light a cigarette. Kaboom! Similar explosions have happened around the country, so stay safe, little cookers, and for God's sake use the common sense you were born with and don't smoke in the presence of highly flammable gases.

Because Ear Wax is so potent, there have also been a few reports of people freaking out after smoking it, especially the first time. Apparently, the hallucinogenic properties of cannabis are intensified with the high THC content, and the high lasts much longer than usual, so some people end up tripping balls in the worst way. But like any other drug, it's about knowing your limits and using in moderation. Keep in mind that, medically, Ear Wax is used for those with extreme symptoms or a high tolerance to bud, so treat it accordingly and with respect.

INDEX

PICTURE CREDITS

All images are copyright their respective copyright holders and are shown here for historical and review purposes. Every effort has been made to credit the copyright holders, artists and/or studios/publishers whose work has been reproduced in these pages. We apologize for any omissions, which will be corrected in future editions, but must hereby disclaim any liability.

© Roman Sigaev *p2* / © Hein Nouwens *p9* / © Atomazul *p14* / © Daniel J. Rao *p18* / *Marijuana Girl* © 1951 Universal Publishing, New York *p21* / *Marihuana* © 1941 Detective Fiction Weekly, Dell Publishing *p31* / © Featureflash *p34* / Library of Congress, Washington D.C. *p38* / © Lucian Coman *p54* / © aastock *p60* / © Carl Van Vechten, Library of Congress, Washington D.C. *p66* / © Eldad Carin *p75* / *Junkie: Confessions of an Unredeemed Drug Addict* © Ace Books, New York *p88* / © Steven Bostock *p93*